The New York Harbor Book

The New York Harbor Book

by Francis J. Duffy
and William H. Miller

TBW Books   Falmouth, Maine

Frontis: American Export's largest passenger liners, the sister ships *Constitution* (shown) and *Independence,* were two of the most popular ships to sail from the Port of New York.

Cover photo: The schooner *Pioneer,* out of the South Street Seaport Museum, sails past the Statue of Liberty on a harbor cruise. (Photo F.J.D.)

TBW Books, 36 Old Mill Road, Falmouth, Maine 04105
© 1986 by Francis J. Duffy & William H. Miller
All rights reserved. Published 1986
Printed in the United States of America
ISBN 0-931474-33-7 Hardbound
ISBN 0-931474-34-5 Paperback

To the Great Lady of the Port of New York and New Jersey, the Statue of Liberty, on her hundredth birthday, October 28, 1986.

INTRODUCTION I

It was one of those moments that has never faded from my memory, during a walk with my father across the recently opened Triborough Bridge. Looking down from the walkway, 315 feet above the East River and infamous Hell Gate waters, I watched the ships and boats pass below and confidentially told my father that when I grew up, I wanted to work on ships. At that moment I fell under a nautical spell, and like my co-author, Bill Miller, I am still enthralled with the maritime world.

The days of World War II were exciting ones for the Port of New York and New Jersey, some of the busiest, for traffic, that the harbor would ever see. I watched this great drama from the shores of Astoria Park, near my home, overlooking the Hell Gate waters. All sorts of ships and boats sailed to and from Long Island Sound, taking the longer route than by ocean, but a safer one, away from the danger of submarines, especially in the dark days of 1943. I could listen to the lookout on the Triborough Bridge send instructions down to the ships by a loud-speaker above the noise of the traffic.

It was at this time that I saw my first Liberty ship dock in Pots Cove, a pier that has now succumbed to the advance of landfill. The Navy PT boats would race through the Gate, their gasoline engines roaring, testing their speed before going off to war. The panorama of vessels was endless; tankers, cargo ships, military vessels, tugs, barges, and railroad carfloats, enough to hold a young boy's attention for hours on end and encourage him to build dreams of sailing away some day.

The war ended before I reached the age to ship out, but I did fulfill my boyhood dream after high school, sailing in the merchant marine on tankers, Liberty ships, troop transports, and even refugee carriers. Although the romance of the sea paled after I was married and had children, even after swallowing the anchor and coming ashore to work, my fascination with things maritime has never ended.

Over the ensuing years my writing and photography have

taken me on a variety of assignments in the world of ships and the sea. I visited oil rigs out in the Atlantic Ocean, sailed on a square-rigger, climbed to the tops of lighthouses, flew over ice floes in a helicopter. I rode on Coast Guard cutters, schooners, fishing boats, pilot boats, police launches, tugboats, and maritime college training ships, and landed to explore the deserted islands of the harbor. The vessels, places, and mostly the people of my New York and New Jersey homeports became my primary beat.

Bill Miller and I wrote this book to share this fascinating world, both past and present, with our readers.

Valley Stream, N.Y.   Francis James Duffy
January 1985

INTRODUCTION II

THEY WERE MAGICAL times, summer afternoons mostly—the river was alive with craft; horns and whistles honked and screeched, and the salt smell was blended with whiffs of hemp, tar, oil, and rubber. My special vantage point was a near-deserted Lackawanna ferry, diligently working its way back and forth between Hoboken and Lower Manhattan's Barclay Street in those somnolent hours between the heavy commuter rushes. An elderly, often stooped shoeshine vendor was sometimes the only other passenger. The captain and his mate were above, in one of those secluded wheelhouses (there was one at each end) on the uppermost deck; the engine crews seemed to live secretly down below.

The New York skyline was, in those years—the fifties and early sixties—more distinctive, without the wide, obliterating steel and glass box towers of today's urban landscape. The older spires pointed skyward regally; the city was the kingdom. They seemed to look down upon the harbor and its darting, steaming, criscrossing ships and boats with a warm benevolence. Downtown were the serenity of the Woolworth Building and the sleek, slender, depression style of the Cities Service and Bank of Manhattan towers. The New York Telephone Building, an imposing block of red-brown, stood at the waterfront, just above the Lackawanna ferry terminal. It seemed to grow to enormous size as we approached the city and then, steaming back to the Jersey side, it would begin to regain proportion, shrink somewhat and melt again into the total skyline. The openness of midtown New York began with the Metropolitan Life tower and was capped by the most visible of all, the Empire State Building, surrounded by the Chrysler and RCA buildings, as well as other lesser skyscrapers.

The Lackawanna ferry captains made their way with skill and precision. Smaller craft avoided these determined, often rushing vessels, which in turn would alter their course to skirt bigger ships, freighters, and liners. Often, we'd pass at least one other ferry, making the opposite run. Tugboats, with names and smokestack insignias of such firms as Moran, Dalzell, Red Star, and Turecamo seemed to be everywhere—speeding off to an assignment or hauling a barge loaded with gravel, freight cars, or trash. Others might be assisting an inbound cargo ship. A muscular floating derrick, white steam spouting to a special cadence from her engine house, might be at work with a freighter, lifting aboard a glistening new boiler or a string of locomotives. Some of the midday procession of outbound liners would sail past, bigger than life and lined with the tiny bodies of passengers bound, possibly, for Cherbourg, Bergen, or Naples. Perhaps one of the gigantic Cunard *Queens*, waiting for the appropriate afternoon tide, might be downriver, still in the Lower Bay, about to make her final passage to an uptown berth.

The green and rusted sheds of the Hudson River piers fed diverse cargoes, in slings and on pallets attached to hooked pulleys, into large freighters: the *President Taft*, bound for Manila; the *Rio Araza*, for Buenos Aires; the *Mormacsaga* for Copenhagen; the *Vinkt* for Boma in the Congo; the *Santa Sofia* for Maracaibo; the *American Trapper* for Antwerp, and a string of American Export ships, like the *Exford* and *Exemplar*, bound for Tripoli or Karachi, just next to the Hoboken ferry terminal.

The New York Harbor of those years was a very busy, exciting, and special place. I am indeed fortunate to have had a front-row seat. Writing this book with Francis Duffy has brought those wondrous times back to life for me.

Jersey City, New Jersey   William H. Miller
January 1985

ACKNOWLEDGMENTS

So many people have helped me prepare and write my chapters of this book that I dare not attempt to mention them all by name. The risk of omitting deserving individuals is all too great. Let me, therefore, simply thank all those in the maritime community who have so generously made me part of their work and their lives, ashore and afloat. I greatly appreciate too the many editors, both here and in the U.K., who saw enough merit in these stories to publish them previously. I owe a special debt to my wife Joan and five children for their help, tolerance, and understanding.

F.J.D.

I would like to note the most important help offered me by Frank O. Braynard (dean of American maritime historians and an inspiration for so many of us), John Catrambone, Fred Rodriguez, Victor Scrivens, Everett E. Viez, and Thomas C. Young. Corporations and organizations that have assisted me include the American Export Lines, Bethlehem Steel Company, French Line, Furness-Bermuda Line, Hapag-Lloyd, Moore McCormack Lines, Moran Towing & Transportation Company, the Port Authority of New York & New Jersey, Sea-Land Service, Steamship Historical Society of America, Todd Shipyards, Incorporated, and the United States Lines.

W.H.M.

CONTENTS

A pilot is being transferred to the ship he will guide.

I WORKING and WATCHING the PORT F.J.D.

LONG BEFORE a landfall is made, when a ship is within twenty-five miles of the pilot station boat at the Port of New York and New Jersey, a call is made via the ship's VHF radio to the Sandy Hook Pilots. The ship gives her estimated time of reaching the pilot station and receives instructions as to which side of the ship the pilot will board. This first contact will start a chain of events bringing into play all the government and private groups that make the port operate.

The Sandy Hook Pilots

"Always on Station," is the motto of the Sandy Hook Pilots, whose official name is the United New York and United New Jersey Sandy Hook Pilots Benevolent Associations. After several ship disasters in the last century resulted in heavy loss of life, due to not having an experienced pilot on board, both New York and New Jersey passed legislation requiring, with few exceptions, the use of pilots on vessels coming and going from the port. One of the station boats, *New York Pilot #1* or *New Jersey Pilot #2*, is always either anchored or cruising at the entrance of the harbor, placing pilots on ships arriving, or picking up those who have just brought a ship out of the harbor. The station boats have black hulls, and printed in large yellow letters on both sides are the words "Pilot 1" or "Pilot 2."

The port's pilots trace their origins back to 1694 when New York State passed its first law for pilotage. In history, statutory injunctions date back to Roman and Hanseatic ordinances for pilots. Like many of the port's professionals, pilots have a tradition of service that goes back more than a hundred years.

The "Hook Pilots," as they are known in the port, number about a hundred. They handle some five hundred ship movements a month, twenty-four hours a day, seven days a week. The career of a pilot starts when he receives an appointment as an apprentice. Most of the apprentices have fathers or other close relatives who are pilots. I have never seen a more disciplined group than these men, many of whom have already graduated from college and in addition have been officers on seagoing ships. They start out working on the station boats and running the 40-foot motorboats that transfer the pilots. This period, which is also spent in studying for various Coast Guard licenses, takes about three and a half years. Another four years is needed to obtain the necessary State Pilot licenses. Before a pilot reaches the status of Branch Pilot, he has had a combined apprentice training and deputy piloting of fifteen years. The term "branch" comes from the Fourteenth Century in England. It refers to a man who has passed all the requirements and is able to pilot any size ship.

When a ship comes into the vicinity of the Ambrose Light Station, at the entrance to the harbor, the Hook Pilot swings aboard one of the motorboats that will transfer him from the station boat to the incoming ship, which has slowed down for his arrival. Depending on the size and type of ship, a side port is opened in the hull, or a Jacob's ladder, a non-rigid ladder with ropes or chains for the sides and steps of wood or metal, is lowered, often hanging thirty feet down the side of the ship. When the sea is rough, especially in winter months, boarding a ship this way is a dangerous and tricky feat. When the motorboat reaches the side of the ship the pilot has to time the motion of the waves and jump for the ladder on the crest. There's really only one chance at the ladder, and there's always the danger of missing and falling into the sea, or worse yet, getting caught between the motorboat and the side of the ship. Even when the pilot has reached the top of the ladder and climbed over the ship's rail he may still have to go as many as seven decks up to the ship's bridge. Having followed one of the pilots on an Ambrose boarding on a relatively tranquil summer day, I always marvel at their doing it, night and day, twelve months a year. A study made in the United Kingdom, measuring stress on harbor pilots, found that one of the highest heartbeat rates was experienced while boarding and disembarking from a ship.

When the pilot reaches the bridge, the ship's captain knows he is in good hands as they enter the main Ambrose Channel, named for Dr. John Wolfe Ambrose, an Irish physician and engineer who lobbied eighteen years to get Congress to appropriate money for the channel, but died before it was dredged. The pilot will call out the compass headings to the helmsman at the wheel

2

of the ship, keeping her safely in deep water. The channel, which starts some twenty-five miles from the tip of Manhattan, is two thousand feet wide and forty-five feet deep. The completion of it in 1907 assured that the port would remain the nation's number one seaport. The *Lusitania* was the first ship to use the Ambrose Channel inbound, in 1907.

The Maritime Association of the Port of New York and New Jersey

While the Hook Pilot is guiding a ship into port, a great many other people are also interested in her, making sure that she arrives safely and remains secure. Marine intelligence, a term that seems to be left over from World War II, is actually a collection of data on all ships entering and leaving the port. Since 1873 this data has been compiled and supplied by some 140 member firms of the Maritime Association of the Port of New York and New Jersey founded at 61 Beaver Street in lower Manhattan.

From the early days of the port, transmittal of ship movements has been valuable to many firms, as well as government agencies concerned with seagoing traffic. Ships will need bunkers (fuel for the engines), food, repairs, crew changes, pilot services, and tugs. At first, a crude system of semaphore flags mounted on high poles was used to relay the arrival of ships off Sandy Hook. This system was later improved by the use of telegraph and then consolidated into what was first called the Maritime Exchange.

The Association's membership and activities grew with the port and came to include other endeavors such as port promotion. Today the Maritime Association still maintains a lookout at its headquarters at 17 Battery Place, at the tip of Manhattan. The tenth floor control room overlooks the upper bay, and is tied into the communication network of the maritime world of pilots, U.S. Coast Guard, and subscribers by teletype, VHF-FM radio, and computers.

The lookout on duty, twenty-four hours a day, seven days a week, answers the phone with information for members, checks the harbor waters with binoculars for the location of ships, mans the VHF radio, and types information into the computer for use of the Association's twelve hundred subscribers. The computer screen shows all the available information about each ship in port: type, flag of nationality, cargo, last port of call, and destination

The lookout on duty in the Maritime Association's control room computerizing all available information on ships in port.

in the harbor, or the next port of call (when outbound). Shipping agencies receive radiograms from the ships while they're still far out to sea, estimating their time of arrival and what services are needed. This data is then relayed via the Association to interested parties.

Aids-to-Navigation

There isn't a boat or ship that travels the waters of the port and the Hudson River as far as Albany that doesn't depend on aids to navigation for a safe passage. These aids, lighthouses, buoys, and day-markers have been the responsibility of the U.S. Coast Guard since 1936, when it took over the duties of the old U.S. Lighthouse Service. The tending of the more than four hundred navigational aids is the main mission of USCGC *Red Beech*, a 115-foot buoy tender based at the Coast Guard's headquarters on Governors Island, New York. The little black-hulled vessel and her thirty-man crew carry out this mission alone.

Red Beech is designed on the lines of the old Lighthouse Service tenders, her captain, Lt. Robert Papp, USCG, told me while I sailed aboard as an observer. The boat works a twelve-hour day to keep up with maintenance of the various aids. Routine maintenance calls for an annual check that each aid is in the right location; an inspection of the concrete anchor and chain; and hauling the buoys for checking and painting. In addition, the boat supplies the few lighthouses that are still manned. Like all Coast Guard vessels, *Red Beech* will answer calls for search and rescue and even carry out law enforcement duties. It's one of the big jobs the smallest of our armed services, the U.S. Coast Guard, performs, without which the port could not function.

The buoy tender U.S. Coast Guard Cutter *Red Beech* is responsible for all the aids-to-navigation in the port as well as in the Hudson River as far as Albany.

5

U.S. Army Corps of Engineering

The life of the port is dependent on the channels that can handle deep-draft ocean ships as well as provide for the safe passage of smaller vessels, and this job is one of the chief responsibilities of the U.S. Army Corps of Engineers. The Corps, with a fleet of civilian-crewed, special boats and outside contractors, dredges the channels, clears the waters of driftwood and other debris, and checks against polluters on the federal waterways.

The role of the Army in the ports of the nation dates from 1775, a year before the Declaration of Independence, when General George Washington assigned a deputy to plan the defenses of New York harbor against British attack. The New York District of the Corps is responsible for navigation in Lake Champlain, the Hudson River, New York Harbor, and Long Island Sound. During the War of 1812 the Corps built a series of forts around the port. Many, such as Forts Totten, Wadsworth, Jay, Williams, and Schuyler, are still harbor landmarks today.

In 1885 a reef and rock in the Hell Gate waters that had caused many shipwrecks was removed by the Army Corps and thus saved the port from losing its commerce to others on the East Coast. In war and peace the Corps of Engineers have supervised the building and protection of the Port of New York and New Jersey.

The *Hayward*'s mission is to keep the port waters free of debris.

Fireboats

There is no way in which a land-based fire engine could fight or control a fire afloat, or get to a blaze on a finger pier jutting out into the water. It's a credit to early fire fighters that they saw the need for a specialized type of harbor protection. The answer was a "floating engine," a fireboat, with a nozzle delivery rate of water exceeding that of any land-based steam pumper, the mobility to respond to waterfront and ship fires, and the ability to assist fire companies ashore by supplying water.

Volunteer fire fighters in New York are credited with the first fireboat. They mounted a rotary engine on a whaleboat in 1809. The pumper, known as a "coffee mill," was powered by six men on each crank for pumping. The whaleboat needed a crew of twenty-four men to row and operate the pump. The English put the first floating steam engine on the River Thames in 1852. Today most major seaports, like the Port of New York and New Jersey, have fireboats. Thirty-three cities in the United States use marine fire protection units.

In 1874 the Fire Commissioners of New York City gave out a contract for the first full-time, fully-equipped fireboat, the *William F. Havemeyer*. She was a wooden-hull vessel, steam-propelled. The firemen and crew lived aboard. With a pumping capacity of three thousand gallons per minute, the 106-foot long *Havemeyer* was far greater than any other steam pumper of her day. She served the port for twenty-six years.

From 1875, when she was placed in service, the New York fireboat fleet grew with the expanding port. At the turn of the century the city had four boats in service besides the *Havemeyer*: the twin-stack *Zophar Mills*, *William L. Strong*, *Seth Low*, and *David A. Boody*. The latter two started life as citizens of the City of Brooklyn, but were transferred to New York City when the two municipalities were joined together in 1898.

The queen of the fleet for many years, and one of the largest fireboats in the world at the time, was the *New Yorker*, launched in 1891. She was a steel-hulled boat, 125 feet long, powered by an 800-horsepower triple expansion steam engine. The rapid development of marine fire protection could be seen in her pump capacity, 13,000 gallons per minute. She had the further distinction of being the first fireboat to have quarters for the crew ashore.

This boat became a maritime landmark, stationed at the foot of Manhattan, at the Battery, near Castle Garden. It was the *New Yorker* that had the honor of leading the parade of ships in the harbor when the city welcomed Admiral Dewey on his return after the battle of Manila Bay, in the Spanish American War.

Within the first decade of the twentieth century, the marine division of the Fire Department experienced two major harbor disasters that set records that still stand today for loss of life in the port. A fire at the North German Lloyd Line Pier in Hoboken, New Jersey, took four hundred lives on June 30, 1900, and the burning of the excursion steamer *General Slocum* resulted in the loss of one thousand twenty-one lives in 1904.

North German Lloyd Pier Fire

Four German liners were docked in Hoboken on that June Saturday in 1900, the *Kaiser Wilhelm der Grosse, Saale, Main,* and *Bremen.* The piers were packed with bales of cotton, barrels of whiskey, turpentine, oils, and other highly inflammable materials. The ships had also attracted many visitors and were crowded. Fire started in the cotton bales, the cause unknown to this day, and quickly spread to the ships. Land-based fire fighters responded within minutes, but it was too late, for the fire had already engulfed the ships and the wooden Pier 3, and was spreading to adjoining piers and small boats.

Mutual aid pacts are common among many fire departments and, by a long-standing tradition that is still honored today, the New York City fireboats protect the communities in New Jersey that front on the waters of the harbor. When the fire started in Hoboken the alarm brought the boats from the west side of Manhattan. The men aboard could already see the holocaust across the Hudson River in New Jersey. The *Kaiser Wilhelm der Grosse* and the *Bremen* were pushed out into the Hudson, while the *Saale* and the *Main* burned at the dock, along with many small boats and barges. Twenty-eight people from the drifting, flame-driven *Bremen* were saved by the *New Yorker,* but seventy-four people died on that ship alone.

The General Slocum Disaster

The side-wheel excursion steamer *General Slocum* was chartered to St. Mark's Church on the lower east side of Manhattan when she sailed for a picnic grove on Long Island Sound on June 16, 1904. The boat caught fire in the East River, off the shore of Queens, just before starting the infamous Hell Gate passage. The

Above: No photographers were present when the *General Slocum* burned on the shore of North Brother Island in June 1904, but an artist tried to convey the horror of it. *Below:* Survivors of the catastrophe await help.

captain, fearing the currents, whirlpools, and rocks of Hell Gate, pushed the burning boat on to beach her on North Brother Island. The fireboats never had a chance to fight the fire on the *General Slocum* before it had taken the lives of 1,021 passengers, mostly women and children. When the Chief of the Department, Edward F. Crocker, reached the scene aboard the *Zophar Mills*, the only job left was to recover the many bodies floating in the river in the vicinity of the Bay of the Brothers.

The Ammunition Ship El Estero

World War II saw the greatest concentration of traffic in the port's history. Half of all the troops and a third of all the supplies sent overseas in World War II passed through the port. When the nation entered the war, the fireboat fleet changed its livery from red and white to battleship gray. In the early days of the war, before the Navy and Coast Guard had the boats or personnel, the fireboats became the first line of defense patrolling the port against sabotage. They covered the sailings of all major troop ships and had on board the plans of all the ships using the harbor, so that they could know the location of the ammunition magazines.

The major depot for the shipping of ammunition through the port during World War II was Caven's Point Terminal, Jersey City, near the Statue of Liberty. On April 24, 1943, the Panamanian freighter *El Estero* was loading a cargo of ammunition, bombs, and other high explosives, including a deck cargo of drums of high octane aviation gasoline. In spite of the most elaborate fire protection and security on the pier and aboard the ships at Caven's Point, a fire started on *El Estero*. An oil burner on a boiler had a flashback, which in turn ignited some oil in the ship's bilge in the engine room. The fire spread quickly on the cargo ship and, unless she were moved, it would carry over to other ships at the dock and to the stored ammunition ashore, which, in turn, could cause a chain reaction along the New Jersey waterfront, oil tank farms, and refineries.

The city fireboat *Firefighter* was called to the scene, and she was placed in a situation that few combat vessels of World War II ever faced. She was lashed up to the burning *El Estero*, and while pouring water into the ship, started to move it away from the dock. The danger was so great to the port area that the radio stations requested people to leave their windows open and stay clear because of the fear of a blast. With the help of civilian tugs and Coast Guard boats, *El Estero* was moved to a point off Robbins Reef Lighthouse, near St. George, Staten Island, and sank. It was said that after the sinking the waters belched with many explosions. The New York City Fire Department awarded decorations to twenty-six firemen from the *Firefighter* and the *John J. Harvey,* for the part they played in minimizing the damage from the *El Estero* fire.

The *Firefighter,* which replaced the *New Yorker* in the city's fleet (these two boats are the only ones not named to honor members of the department), is still in service. Designed by the firm of Gibbs & Cox, the same firm that designed the Liberty ship of World War II and the luxury liners *America* and *United States,* the twin-screw, Diesel electric boat was built at United Shipyard, Staten Island, at a cost of $924,000 in 1938. The 134-foot fireboat can throw out sixteen thousand gallons of water a minute at 150 pounds per square inch of pressure from her cannons and hoses. Today the *Firefighter* is stationed at Marine Company 9, near the Staten Island ferry slip at St. George.

In recent years, since World War II, the Marine Division has continued to protect the port. Many events have proven its effectiveness and the bravery of the boat crews. When, on June 2, 1972, the containership *Sea Witch* collided with the fully loaded oil tanker *Esso Brussels,* which was at anchor near the Verrazano Bridge, a spectacular fire resulted. The *Firefighter* moved into the burning oil to rescue thirty crew members trapped on the burning tanker. This collision and fire took sixteen lives and did $50 million damage.

At the tip of Manhattan, at the west end of the Battery sea wall, is Pier A, North River. It was built in 1885, and is one of the most beautiful piers in the harbor, with a red, gray, and green building and stone arches in the foundation. A seventy-foot clock tower, which was added in 1918, is a memorial to the nation's dead of World War I, and has the distinction of being one of the three public clocks in the country that toll the time in ship's bells. This landmark pier, saved for preservation in 1977, is the headquarters for the Marine Division.

Today the division has an annual budget of $5 million, but this pays for a smaller fleet of boats and crews than at any time since the turn of the century. Only four marine companies protect the port, and they cover only the central harbor area. The managers of the Fire Department have taken a calculated risk in not having boats stationed near the fishing fleet of Sheepshead Bay, or the outlying marinas of City Island.

A Typical Fireboat Display

One of the most impressive public-relations functions of the New York City fireboats is the water display they put on for maiden arrivals of ships to the port and for special harbor events. Few seaports can match the sight of a fireboat sending up plumes of water in the traditional New York welcome off the Battery, with the Manhattan skyline in the background. During harbor events, such as Operation Sail 1976, and at the annual Harbor Festival, dye is added to the water so that the spray comes out red, white, and blue.

Policing the Port

Keeping law and order on the waters of the port is one of the jobs of the New York City Police Department's Harbor Patrol Unit. Back in 1858 this unit was first organized with twelve rowboats to fight river pirates who had been terrorizing the waterfront. The rowboats were replaced when the Marine Division put its first steamboat in service in 1863, a side-wheeler, the *Seneca*. The steamboat served the unit until replaced by gasoline powered boats in 1926. These, in turn, were replaced by Diesel launches, similar to those still in use today.

All the policemen assigned to the Harbor Unit are volunteers. Besides being qualified patrolmen, they have had additional experience in marine work, such as the Navy, Coast Guard, merchant marine, or commercial fishing. Like their counterparts ashore, they patrol posts in the harbor waters that are referred to by phonetic names: Harbor Adam, Boy, Charlie, and George. The patrol boats, mostly 52-foot launches, operate twenty-four hours a day, seven days a week, all year round. The boats are painted in the same blue and white livery as squad police cars ashore.

The New York City Police Department's launch *Harbor Charlie* patrols the East River.

When spring comes to the port the warming waters give up the bodies of victims of homicides, suicides, and drownings. It is the job of the Harbor Unit to recover these bodies, or "floaters," brought to the surface by decaying bacteria, which form gas. There are generally one hundred and fifty to two hundred bodies recovered each year. When the location of a body is known, grappling hooks are used. One of the saddest duties these patrolmen perform is bringing up the body of a young child.

One of the most unusual units in the Police Department, the Underwater Recovery team, is attached to the Harbor Unit. This is an organization of scuba divers, all trained outside the department, who dive in the harbor waters for bodies or suspected evidence of crime such as guns, jewelry, and stolen cars. The harbor waters are so dark and murky that visibility is only a few inches and the divers work mostly by feel. Diving in the harbor waters also carries the risk of serious infection from pollution.

The U.S. Park Police

When the Federal Government established the Gateway National Recreation area, the need arose for a special police unit to protect and enforce laws, and a marine unit was formed. Although much smaller than the New York City Police Harbor Unit, the Park Police still have responsibility for sixteen thousand acres of waterways, marshlands, offshore islands, and the shorelines on Jamaica, Raritan, and Sandy Hook bays. Since some fifty percent of this area is submerged land, only a marine unit could provide proper coverage.

The Park Police patrol with inboard Diesel skiffs and two outboard high-speed boats. All the men in the marine unit are licensed motorboat operators, having passed the U.S. Coast Guard tests, and are also certified Emergency Medical Technicians. Four of the officers are qualified scuba divers. The urban park lands are heavily used in summer months, with much of that use being by pleasure boaters. During the off season, the Park Police put on educational programs for city schools and give lectures on boating and water safety at yacht clubs. Like all the units in the harbor, they work and cooperate with the N.Y. City Police, Coast Guard, U.S. Fish and Wildlife Service, and the N.Y. State Conservation Department—all government agencies that maintain patrol boats in the harbor waters.

14

Managing the Waterfront

The 1980s have seen major changes in the shorelines of the Port Authority of New York & New Jersey with two agencies sharing the responsibility, the New York City's Department of Ports & Terminals and the Port Authority of New York & New Jersey. The city agency concerns itself with the shore line within the city limits, while the Port Authority is a bi-state agency. Between these two bodies, and with the input of local communities, the piers and terminals are built and managed, although for the most part operated by private companies.

The present Ports & Terminals Department goes back more than a century ago when it was the Department of Docks, Ports & Terminals. Nothing happens along the city waterfront with which this department doesn't concern itself: restaurants on the water, fishing fleet docks in Sheepshead Bay, Bay Street Landing, residential development on Staten Island, and the maritime museums. While many of the industrial facilities have left the waterfront, a gentrification trend is now gaining strength. Ports & Terminals has to investigate all plans, issue permits, and do engineering studies. This department operates with all the pressures and politics of the city. It is a credit to the agency that it has accomplished so much.

The Port Authority of New York & New Jersey was founded in 1921 to help bring order to the chaos of the time between the two states, the railroads, and other pressure groups. The Authority was modeled after the Port of London Authority and is supervised by a board of unpaid commissioners, six appointed by each state. Its mission is defined simply as promoting the commerce of the port. It controls and operates seven marine terminals, including the largest container terminals in the world at Port Newark and Port Elizabeth and at Howland Hook, Staten Island, recently taken over from New York City. These were built just in time to take care of the containerization revolution of ocean-going cargo and are one of the main reasons the port is the nation's number one seaport. Besides the marine terminals, the Port Authority has built many of the port's landmarks: the twin towers of the World Trade Center, George Washington Bridge, three other bridges, three major airports, two bus terminals, and two tunnels under the Hudson River.

Voyaging to the Dead Sea

Early settlers in the port area saw the rivers and bays not only as a means of transportation but also a natural way of carrying away the wastes of civilization. It was not uncommon, as late as 1934, to dump the garbage off scows at the entrance to the harbor; some sewer pipes still empty into the rivers. Pollution filled the harbor waters before it was discovered that this was not the way to dispose of waste. Now communities along the waterfront have adopted alternative methods and have passed strict laws against violators.

The tanker *North River* is a familiar sight in the waters of the port, but few people outside the maritime and environmental communities know of her important mission. She flies the American flag, unfortunately seldom seen on an ocean-going tanker in the port these days, and carries the blue and orange colors and the shield of the City of New York on her funnel. This gray-hulled, spotless white superstructured tanker is seen on the average of four times a day, in all seasons, traveling at a brisk pace in different parts of the rivers and bays of the port. *North River* is the newest and largest of the New York City's four-ship fleet of tank-

The tanker MV *North River* rushes to keep up with the removal of sludge from New York City.

ers that transport sludge from the city's sewage-treatment plants to the ocean dumping grounds, more commonly known as the "Dead Sea." Besides *North River*, New York City's Environmental Protection Agency operates the tankers *Owls Head*, *Bowery Bay*, and *Newtown Creek*, each named for one of the sewage plants the fleet services.

New York City has used this method of sludge disposal for some forty-five years, a fact seldom mentioned by critics of the city, and has been a pioneer in sewage treatment. On a typical day *North River* will load a cargo of 180,000 cubic feet of wet sludge at one of the treatment plants and sail for the dumping grounds. A special "black box," installed in the ship and supervised by the U.S. Coast Guard, monitors the dumping of the sludge as to time, location, and amount.

The crews of the tankers are all Coast Guard certified and licensed for ocean-going ships, and are employed as civil servants by the city. The tankers load at ten treatment plants in the city's five boroughs. The run to the dumping site takes about two hours, with the ships hitting a top speed of fourteen knots. The dumping of the eight tanks is done by gravity from a manifold on the bridge, after which the tanks are flushed with sea water. The thing that stands out when watching the dump is how the wake of the tanker turns from a normal white to jet black.

The Marine Protection, Research and Sanctuaries Act of 1972 mandated that the dumping of the sludge just twelve miles out must stop, but the city has fought the law in the courts. The plan is to move the dumping site still farther out to sea, some one hundred miles. The longer trip will increase fivefold the cost of disposal for the city. Over the years the sludge tanker crews have become veterans of the many studies and coverage by the press and take it all in stride, even when many stories single out the seamen as the villains of the environment. As one crew member remarked to me when I made the trip to the Dead Sea, "No one can come out of sludge smelling like roses."

Tugboats

In 1979, when the union representing the crews on the harbor tugs and barges went on strike, the people in the port area once again learned that their daily lives still depend heavily on harbor workers. Garbage piled up in the streets, for the tugs were not available to move the scows that carried the garbage to the landfill areas. Power plants that depend on the delivery of oil by barge faced using more expensive truck deliveries. The five hundred ships that come and go into the port were required to dock without the assistance of tugs. More than any other vessels in the port's home fleet, the tugboats keep the harbor going.

"Seventeen to the Dorothy: Drop a line on the Margaret." These calls that go out on the VHF-FM Marine radio have nothing to do with girls, but come from the dispatchers of the Moran Towing and Transportation Company. Moran, which was founded by an Irish immigrant in 1860, is one of the leaders in the towing industry in the port, and is still headed by a fourth-generation family member, Thomas E. Moran. The "seventeen" in the radio call is a carry-over from the days when the company had offices at 17 Battery Place, and the girls' names are those of family members used for the boats.

At one time the harbor waters were filled with tugboats, powered by steam engines and owned by the railroads and even by individuals, but those days are long past. Today there are three major companies operating in the port, Moran, McAllister, and

The tugboat *Margaret Moran* pushes up against the bow of a ship while docking her.

18

Turecamo. The railroad fleets are long gone, and the small vessels have Diesel power plants of up to 6,000 horsepower. Although tugs still dock ships, more of their work is in transporting fuel by barges that are bigger than the ships of the past. There is no vessel in the port so recognizable to the lay person as the tugboat.

On the Spiritual Side

Father Lee Smith, a priest in the Roman Catholic Diocese of Brooklyn, seldom sees the same people two Sundays in a row, or says Mass in the same place. His parish is the Brooklyn waterfront, the Mass is said aboard ships in port, and his parishioners are their crews. The center for Father Smith's work is a small red brick building near the Port Authority's Pier 9, Brooklyn, at Degraw and Van Brunt streets, the Stella Maris Seaman's Center. The Apostleship of the Sea, an international organization of the Catholic Church ministering to seafarers, was founded in Scotland in 1922 and came to the United States during World War II.

The services provided by Father Smith at the Center are both spiritual and temporal. One of the major attractions that draw seamen to the center is the availability of phone service for overseas calls, at a cheaper rate and with more privacy than public booths. The facility also has a place to watch TV, write a letter home, or shoot a game of pool; and the ever-welcome pot of coffee is always on. Most of the men and women who come to the Center are crews from Third World countries and those of the flag-of-convenience vessels, who work for low wages and welcome the free clothes donated. Father Smith often doubles as a chauffeur for visiting seamen, taking them shopping in the Center's van to places that offer the best buys for their limited budgets. Although many of the crews are Catholics, the center welcomes all seafarers.

Seaman's Church Institute

The Episcopal Church has served seafarers coming to the Port of New York and New Jersey since it started a floating chapel in 1834. Over the years the Seaman's Church Institute has become a home away from home for seafarers of all nationalities and creeds. Visitors from the SCI go aboard ships in port, even if the ships stay only a few hours, offering a wide range of services.

The SCI has an office at 50 Broadway, in Manhattan, and a Center for Seafarers at Port Newark's Container Terminal. Five chaplains offer counseling, and there is also a marine school at the Manhattan location. Volunteers at these locations host dances and soccer matches at Newark, and just simply offer a place in which to relax ashore.

One recent operation of both the Protestant and Catholic seamen's clubs has been a joint effort to protect seafarers' rights. The major maritime countries have their seafarers covered with protective laws and union contracts, but those on the flags-of-convenience vessels, with many of the crews from Third World countries, are at the mercy of the captains and owners. Chaplains act as representatives for seamen who are far from home and often ignorant of their rights. The general public sailing on cruise ships is too often unaware of the working conditions under which foreign crews labor.

The Fresnel Lens on the West Bank Lighthouse

II THE LIGHTS THAT NEVER FAIL
F.J.D.

IT WOULD BE impossible to have an interest in the Port of New York and New Jersey and not include lighthouses, for they are one of the most romantic elements of the maritime world. The use of lighthouses to guide and warn mariners goes back to the reign of Ptolemy II from 283–247 B.C., when the Egyptians built a tower on the small Island of Pharos off Alexandria. Today many of the port's lighthouses have been relegated to non-operational status and dropped from the official light lists, remaining only as static maritime landmarks. Most of the lights still operational are fully automated and no longer have the national ensign flying from a flagpole. The functions of the keepers of years past are carried out by mechanical and electronic means.

The Fresnel Lens

There are few people who have made so great an impact on coastal navigation and piloting as has Jean Austin Fresnel. One of the leaders in Pharology (the science of lighthouse engineering, which takes its name from the earliest known light), Fresnel invented a cut-glass lens that is used in lighthouses the world over. The lens incorporates a system of prisms, focusing the beam of light. Until this lens was developed, the distance a light could be seen at sea totally depended on the height of the lighthouse. Present-day lights are rated in order of Fresnel lens used, going from the first order, which is the largest, down to the sixth and smallest.

The stories that follow of lighthouses in the port were gleaned by traveling about its waters, having obtained the privilege from the Coast Guard of visiting the lights and talking to the few keepers still left. Because of the system of rotation used by the U.S. Coast Guard for assigning people to the lighthouses, many of the individuals mentioned may have gone on to new duties. I also delved back into history for some of the facts and folklore.

The Coney Island Light Station

When Frank Schubert led me up the eighty-seven steps on the circular staircase of the Coney Island Lighthouse he gave no indication of his sixty-plus years. Mr. Schubert is the last of his profession in the United States, a civilian lighthouse keeper, a civil service employee since 1937 of the U.S. Coast Guard, the agency that has responsibility for most of the aids-for-navigation in the country. He's been keeper at the Coney Island Light since 1960, and really has no intention of retiring.

The light is one of many that guide mariners around the shores of the Port of New York and New Jersey. Besides having a civilian keeper, this station is also unique in that it isn't automated. Most of the lighthouses now run by the U.S. Coast Guard are fully automatic, having been converted under the service's LAMP (Lighthouse Automation and Modernization Program).

Although not open to the public, Coney Island Light is easy to visit with the permission of the Coast Guard. It is located on Norton Point, at the tip of Coney Island, in Brooklyn. It's not a very big light, just a 75-foot steel tower with a 70,000 candle power red Fresnel lens. Mr. Schubert lives with his wife in a government-owned Cape Cod house, built in 1890. Over the years this six-room house has seen the three Schubert children grow to adulthood and leave the community of Sea Gate to start lives on their own.

The Fire Island Lighthouse

From 1826 to 1974, when it was extinguished by the Coast Guard and a smaller, weaker light substituted for it on top of a nearby water tower, the Fire Island Lighthouse and its 168-foot tower, off the eastern shore of Long Island, made the first landfall for ships coming to New York from Europe. It was an impressive light with its tower, built in 1858, and a large building to house keepers at the base. Serving as a guide to local boatmen on Great South Bay for one hundred and sixteen years, Fire Island Light never failed to send out a white flash of welcome to immigrants and other travelers to New York once every minute from sunset to sunrise.

Captain Frank Schubert, at the Coney Island Light, is the last civilian lighthouse keeper in the country.

The years have not been kind to the old tower and keepers' quarters, but it once again has a future, thanks to a group of preservationists. In 1982 the Fire Island Lighthouse Preservation Society was formed as a not-for-profit organization with the aim of rebuilding and relighting the light. It is now part of the Fire Island National Seashore and is included in the National Register of Historic Sites. It is the aim of the organization to have the tower completed and the beacon relighted by 1986.

Montauk Point Lighthouse

Paul and Linda Driscoll spend part of their leisure time rebuilding their home, which was built in 1860. This would not be an unusual hobby for a young couple but for the fact that the house is the outermost structure on the eastern tip of Long Island, part of the Montauk Point Light Station. The Montauk Point Light was commissioned by General George Washington in 1797 and has served mariners ever since. Paul Driscoll, a chief boatswain's mate in the U.S. Coast Guard, lives at the light with his family as the officer in charge.

Besides acting as a navigation light, Montauk is also very important to local sport and commercial fishermen and pleasure boaters. A Coast Guardsman is on duty twenty-four hours a day, watching out for all those in local waters. When the Coast Guard tried to automate the light some years ago, in an economy move, local people made a protest march in the dark of night, carrying candles, flashlights, and torches to show their support for the light. The move was rescinded by the Coast Guard. Many small boats have only the foghorn and light from Montauk to guide them to port safely.

In addition to the normal duties of a lighthouse keeper, Paul Driscoll and his crew also run tours of the station in summer months, when as many as three hundred and eighty thousand people visit the area. Located in the Montauk State Park, which is a haven for surf fishermen and campers, the eastern end of Long Island is a prime tourist attraction.

Besides his Coast Guard and family duties—the Driscolls have two children—Chief Driscoll also runs a lighthouse museum in his spare time. His aim is to collect memorabilia and artifacts from the station and nearby that highlight the area's fishing and boating tradition. There's a lot more to Montauk Light than what most mariners see some nineteen miles offshore, the limit of its beacon.

Coney Island Light

The Navesink Light

The first light to have a Fresnel lens in the United States was the Navesink Light, a twin tower structure on the New Jersey shore, built in 1862. Navesink was electrified in 1898, and for a time had a 25,000,000 candle power light, giving its beacon a range only limited by the curvature of the earth. The glow was reportedly seen seventy nautical miles away. The twin towers of Navesink served ships coming to the Port of New York for ninety years, being automated in 1949 and discontinued by the Coast Guard in 1952. Guglielmo Marconi pioneered radio communication at sea from this light station, and during the 1930s radar was developed there. The brownstone twin towers are now a museum, open to the public from May to September, during which time the light is also lit.

Ambrose Light Tower

Boatswain's mate 1st Class John Peterson, USCG, doesn't need to be told that he works at a point in the Atlantic Ocean that averages eight hundred seventy-nine hours of fog between December and March—he has the foghorn droning under him as a constant reminder. Peterson is the officer in charge of the Ambrose Light Station, a Texas-tower that looks like a chair sticking out of the water at the entrance to New York Harbor. A nagivation

The first Fresnel lens used in the United States were in the Navesink Light Towers.

light has been at this point in the Atlantic since 1908, when Ambrose Channel was first dredged and opened to shipping. At first lightships were used to mark the area, but in 1967 the present oil-rig type structure was towed out and placed on station.

The tower is supported by four legs anchored in the sea floor, 170 feet down. Ninety feet above the water's surface is a square house containing the tanks for fuel and water, electronic gear, and living quarters for the Coast Guard crew. On one corner of the 70 × 70 foot roof, which also doubles as a helicopter pad, is a red tower for the six million candle power strobe light that flashes white every 7.5 seconds. Following the tradition of the lightship that the tower replaced, the word ''Ambrose'' is displayed and illuminated on all four sides of the cabin.

Most vessels will be slowing down near the tower to take on a Sandy Hook Pilot, and the Coast Guard crew feels a sense of security knowing that from this point on, the pilots will guide the ships. This offshore aid was built to withstand winds of up to one hundred and fifty miles an hour, but the bent railings are an example of what the angry seas can do. Several times Coast Guard helicopters from Brooklyn Air Station have evacuated personnel from the tower because of the danger of a hurricane, at which time the light is put on automatic.

The Control Room of the Ambrose Lighthouse Tower

The Sandy Hook Lighthouse

In the early 1760s the Colony of New York was developing into a major seaport, but was in danger of losing shipping to other ports because of the number of shipwrecks at the entrance to the harbor. A group of farsighted New York merchants held a lottery and obtained money to build a lighthouse on Sandy Hook. They then levied a tax of twenty-two pence on tonnage entering the harbor, in order to maintain it. It was first called the "New York Light," when put in service on June 11, 1764, but later the name was changed to Sandy Hook. It is one of twelve lighthouses built by the original colonies.

Vessels entering New York Harbor today are still guided by this same light, the oldest original tower still standing and in use in the United States. Although the tower is now farther inland, because of shifting land from ocean currents, it is basically the same as when built by Isaac Conro before the birth of the Republic. Although the light is automated, it is located at the Coast Guard station.

The Romer Shoals Light

There are three hundred eighty-five active lighthouses in the United States, but only fifty-two still have keepers. Automatic lights have had problems, but they save money and eliminate the distasteful assignment of keeper for the Coast Guard. Romer Shoals, one of the first lights encountered at the west side of the Ambrose Channel, is one of many automatic lights in the port. It was named for the pilot boat *William J. Romer*, which struck a submerged wreck and sank, with the loss of one pilot, in 1863.

The West Bank Light

Although lighthouses are often the subject of paintings, the seventy-foot tower of West Bank Light, with its muddy brown color, built on riprap with no outbuildings, generates little interest beyond that of any range light on the Ambrose Channel. The light does, however, still have resident keepers aboard, although it is only a fourth-order Fresnel lens.

Most of the world lives with 90-degree corners, but the space inside West Bank is like a giant tin can. The only difference is that

The constant noise from power generators and air compressors earns short duty periods for the resident keepers on the West Bank Lighthouse.

the circular rooms get smaller as one climbs the traditional stairs from the 38-foot base to the lens room on top. It's a self-contained world, with no outside connections other than by radio. The power for the light comes from a Diesel generator, running twenty-four hours a day, the noise reverberating throughout the steel shell of the tower. In times of fog, the generator is joined by an air compressor that supplies the foghorn, which often drones on for days on end.

Two young Coast Guardsmen work a week aboard the light, return to the station at Sandy Hook for a week, then back to the light for another week, before receiving an extra week's leave, the only consolation for the keeper's duty. West Bank was built in 1901, and it is possible to see the Manhattan skyline and the New Jersey and Long Island shores from the light, but it still doesn't take long to get a feeling of complete isolation, even on a clear day. All the men who work the light agree that the best part of the duty is Tuesday, for that's the day their relief comes out and they can go ashore. (The light was automated in 1985.)

Robbins Reef

The Port of New York and New Jersey has the largest container terminals in the country, and most of these ships dock in New Jersey, or on the west shore of Staten Island. They must sail past the tip of Staten Island out of the main ship channel and off Robbins Reef. On Robbins Reef, which is two miles southwest of the Statue of Liberty in the inner harbor, stands another silent sentinel of the port, Robbins Reef Light, which has been automated since 1965, and is better known by veteran harbor men as "Katie's Light."

Katie Walker came to Robbins Reef in 1885 with her husband and two children, for it was common at the time for keepers to have their families on station. When Katie's husband died, the job as keeper was offered to several male keepers, but they all felt the job too isolated, so Katie Walker, who qualified as an assistant, became keeper of the light in 1895.

For thirty years, the hundred-pound woman, less than five feet tall, tended the light and became a familiar sight to the harbor traffic as she rowed her children to and from school every day, two miles across the water to Staten Island. It was said that Mrs. Walker was terrified of ever visiting Manhattan.

Not only is Katie Walker remembered as one of the famous female lightkeepers, but also for saving an estimated fifty people from the waters around the light. She died in 1930 at the age of eighty-four.

Liberty's Light

Since 1886 a beautiful French lady, the Statue of Liberty, has

The Statue of Liberty's torch was once an aid-to-navigation. The replacement torch, installed in 1985, has no interior light; instead, from July 4, 1986 on, it will be illuminated by spotlights from the outside.

greeted visitors and new citizens to the inner harbor. Few people, however, even in the maritime community of New York, know that the light held in the lady's right hand was for many years an aid-to-navigation and was included in the light list.

From the dedication of the statue in 1886, until 1901, when it was transferred to the then War Department, it was under the jurisdiction of the Lighthouse Board. The years and weather have extracted their toll from the lady's lamp, and it was removed in 1984 as part of the $85 million renovation project for her upcoming birthday, in July of 1986. The replacement lamp will have no interior lights, but will be illuminated by spotlights from the outside.

The Blackwell Light

New York City has always reserved its lesser islands to put away prisoners, the poor, and the chronically ill, and one of the places so used in the last century was Blackwell's Island, in the East River. It has since been renamed Roosevelt Island, and is one of the new towns in the city, but a small lighthouse on its northern tip is a reminder of the past.

The small stone light tower marked the end of Roosevelt Island for vessels passing the northern point and entering the treacherous Hell Gate passage. At the base of the light, which has not been used as an aid since the end of World War II, was a crude inscription carved in rock: "This work was done by John McCarthy, who built this light house from the bottom to the top. All ye who do pass by may pray for his soul when he dies." The light was built around 1872, and legend has it that John McCarthy was one of the patients at a nearby lunatic asylum. Today the little light is a New York City landmark, but the rock on which McCarthy carved his message has been stolen from the base.

The Little Red Lighthouse

When the Port Authority of New York & New Jersey opened the George Washington Bridge in 1932, thus spanning the Hudson River between Manhattan and Fort Lee, New Jersey, there was a small 100-candle powered, red conical light tower, built on Jefferies Hook, under the Manhattan tower of the bridge. New York City had ceded the small plot of land to the Federal Gov-

The small stone tower on the tip of Roosevelt Island is listed as an historic landmark in New York City.

ernment for a light in 1885, but the present tower wasn't built until 1920.

The river pattern has changed over the years and, with the light from the bridge, the U.S. Coast Guard closed the red lighthouse in 1951 and made plans to demolish it. There was a most unexpected public outcry against doing away with it, not from the maritime community, but from thousands of readers of a book about the little light first published in 1942. This was *The Little Red Lighthouse and the Great Gray Bridge,* by Swift and Ward. The land was returned to the city by the Coast Guard, and in the words of the book the Little Red Lighthouse still stands today, ''round and fat, red and jolly and very, very proud.'' In 1982, when the ''Great Gray Bridge'' celebrated its 50th anniversary, the Port Authority's George Washington Bridge staff removed the graffiti and gave the light a new coat of red paint.

Stepping Stones Lighthouse

At the end of the Hell Gate waters, just at the point where the East River ends and Long Island Sound begins, at the back door to the port, is Stepping Stones Lighthouse, built in 1876. The rocks that run from behind the light to the Long Island shores are part of an Indian legend. Evil spirits were said to have driven

The Little Red Lighthouse still stands "round, fat, red and jolly. . . . "

Indians out of New England and they were saved because they could walk across the waters using the "stepping stones."

It's difficult to comprehend, looking at the small house with the built-in light, how the keeper at one time had his family living on the light. Today Stepping Stones still gives off a green beacon, but it, too, has been automated since 1957. The red brick walls of the house, even though located far from the land, are now covered with the urban blight of graffiti inscribed by amphibian vandals.

Execution Rock

One of the last lights in the port area to be automated by the Coast Guard was Execution Rock, at the western end of Long Island Sound. The date in stone over the door of the keeper's house is 1867. Alas, the windows are blocked with stone, since the last keepers left in December of 1979. Execution Rock got its name from the time of the Revolutionary War, when American prisoners of the British were said to have been chained to the rock to die with the incoming tides. The legend had such a hold over keepers that the Lighthouse Service would relieve men who felt uncomfortable with the "ghosts" of the past.

Above: The name Stepping Stones Lighthouse is based on an Indian legend.
Below: Execution Rock Lighthouse

In this aerial view, dating from the mid-fifties, there are eight liners berthed in "Luxury Liner Row": The Home Lines *Italia*, in the lower slip; then three Cunarders, the *Britannic*, *Queen Elizabeth*, and *Mauretania*; the French Line's *Flandre*; the Greek Line's *New York*, which is mostly covered by the terminal building; and, at the far end, Italian Line's *Augustus* and American Export's *Independence*.

III LUXURY LINER ROW W.H.M.

JUST OVER TWO decades ago, the Port of New York had eighteen active passenger piers along its waterfront, or a total of thirty-six active berths. Today, there remain only three passenger piers with six berths!

This tragic decline did not happen overnight. In 1962, passenger ships tied up from one end to the other of Manhattan's fifty or so Hudson River finger piers. Newspaper centerfolds often featured "stackups"—great aerial photos of coincidental gatherings of some of the world's most magnificent ships. The Argentine State Line was the southernmost, at Pier 25, off Franklin Street, just north of the city's financial district. It was followed by Moore-McCormack Lines, at 32 Canal Street, in the shadow of the brown brick ventilator of the Holland Tunnel. Norwegian America and Incres shared Pier 42, at the foot of Morton Street, in Greenwich Village. In the Chelsea section, the Grace Line *Santa* ships used Piers 57 and 58, while farther north, ships of the Zim Lines tied up at Pier 64, at West 24th Street.

Pier 84 at the foot of West 44th Street, was the formal beginning of what was best known as "Luxury Liner Row." Many can recall summer afternoon drives along the old West Side Highway (itself now in the final stages of demolition) when eight or ten liners were moored there, close together. Driving speeds would be reduced, and all eyes would gaze upward, spellbound. The great bows, resting against the bulkheads, the colorful collection of stacks, and the towering masts created an indelible impression.

Pier 84 was also very busy. The four ships of the Italian Line shared it with the three liners of American Export Lines and an occasional freighter. Even the nuclear-powered *Savannah* docked there on her periodic visits to New York. Next door, at Pier 86, were based the super-liner *United States* and her running-mate, *America*.

Pier 88 had three tenants, the French Line, Greek Line, and North German Lloyd. Cunard—then in the waning years of its glorious heyday with no fewer than eight liners—utilized adjoining piers 90 and 92. From the smaller and shorter Pier 95, at West 55th Street, the Furness cruise ships, *Queen of Bermuda* and *Ocean Monarch*, departed on most Saturday afternoons at 3:00 P.M. Pier 97 was the farthest north and the oldest, dating from the 1890s. It handled the liners of Swedish American, Home Lines, Hamburg Atlantic, and National Hellenic American. In winters, it was also host to the Caribbean-bound *Empress* ships of Canadian Pacific.

There was also liner activity on the New Jersey side of the Hudson. The two passenger-cargo ships of the Spanish Line berthed at Harborside Terminal in downtown Jersey City. This terminal had once been the largest cold storage structure in the world. Farther north, at the Hoboken Port Authority piers, center Pier B greeted the American Export combo liners *Excalibur* and *Exeter*. Two blocks farther, Holland-America used two piers for its seven liners and six subsidiary passenger ships.

In far-off Brooklyn, over fifteen transport troopships berthed at Pier 4 of the giant Army Terminal at 58th Street—catering to servicemen, their dependents, and even refugees.

Within a decade, by the early seventies, these passenger operations were either withering or gone without replacement. As a liner port, New York suffered the effects of changing technology. After the first commercial jet crossed to Europe in the autumn of 1958, transatlantic liners began to fall on hard times. In the late fifties, an estimated sixty liners were operating regularly out of New York. As the 1960s unfolded, however, they began to be withdrawn at the rate of five or six a year. Occasionally, they would be accorded a heroine's send-off with saluting fireboats. More often, they left unceremoniously, bound for the scrapyard, unnoticed by those who had admired them so, in their heyday.

Despite board-room optimism, passenger ships—even such greats as the Cunard *Queens* and the *United States*—were soon running in the red. Often, there were more crew members than fare-paying guests on board. When the thirty-one-year-old *Queen Mary* was retired in September of 1967, she had been losing over $2,000,000 a year.

Even the futuristic Pier 40, with three 800-foot berths—built especially for Holland-America off Greenwich Village's West Houston Street—seemed somehow too late. It was closed in 1974, a scant eleven years after opening, and became a storage center and long-term parking lot, and Holland-America moved north to the West Forties.

By the mid-seventies, New York was basically a cruise port—with passenger ships heading off on week-long junkets to Bermuda and the Bahamas, and occasionally on longer runs to the Caribbean. Things were not the same. Gone were the film stars and steamer trunks. Gone was the easy access to Europe by ship. In the winter, it was practically unavailable. The last remaining traditionalist firms, the French, Italian, and Swedish American lines, were pulling out, abandoning their passenger services completely, in the face of rocketing fuel costs and high-priced labor.

By the winter of 1982, even the tropical cruise ship business had abandoned New York. Convenience, creature comfort, and cost accounting had dictated the change. With quick, often inexpensive, air connections to Miami, Port Everglades, and San Juan, harbors that enjoy relatively tropical climates, cruise passengers no longer have to risk cold, stormy voyages south past Cape Hatteras. In these times of high fuel and labor costs, it is far more profitable to base a ship in southern waters, with short distances between ports of call and the kind of weather the passengers are paying for.

In 1973 the Port Authority of New York & New Jersey had leased the former piers 88, 90 and 92 from the city and given them a long overdue facelifting that cost $35 million and included summer cooling and winter heating. This project was never seriously regarded as an incentive to the harbor's liner industry. It was merely a great improvement over existing facilities. When the refurbished terminal, now renamed The Passenger Ship Terminal, was dedicated in November 1974, all other passenger ship piers were closed.

With tenants long gone, there is little interest in those earlier docks. Some have burned—several times over—then have been demolished. Some, like the Grace Line's Pier 58, stood for several years as twisted, neglected, fire-ravaged hulks. The visitors' verandah at the far end of Pier 32 collapsed into the Hudson from erosion. The northern corner of Pier 97 retained a gash made by the *Queen Anna Maria* attempting to dock, without tugs, on a windy morning in the early seventies. The remaining Manhattan piers (excluding The Passenger Ship Terminal, of course) are earmarked for demolition in the years ahead, to make way for the proposed highway and park.

The Passenger Ship Terminal serves largely as a weekend operation during the warmer months. Cruise ships such as the *Homeric*, the *Atlantic*, the *Bermuda Star*, and the *Nordic Prince*, which operate on a weekly schedule, turn around there each weekend from April through October. The *Queen Elizabeth 2,* the last trans-atlantic liner to use New York as her western port, docks at the Terminal. In the winter months, she is employed cruising more tropical waters. Other occasional callers include the *Amerikanis,* the *Galileo,* the *Vera Cruz,* and to a lesser degree, the three cruise ships of the Royal Viking Line.

The Chelsea Piers

Today, the Chelsea piers—Numbers 54 through 62, beginning at Manhattan's West 14th Street—are shabby, pathetic reminders of a glorious past. No ships call there. Only two have any work at all, No. 57 as a city bus storage, and No. 62 as a U. S. Customs

Triumphant and glorious, the *Queen Mary* arrives in New York Harbor on her maiden voyage, in June 1936. Most of the Chelsea Piers, Numbers 56 through 60, can be seen in the background.

impounding station. Decay has set in and is well advanced. Walls and ceilings are collapsing, windows are shattered, and their vast empty spaces echo to the rattling and banging of loose sheet metal and the creaking of timbers, as the winds and tides of the Hudson exert their changing pressures. The only evidence of former glory are faded signs, one offering R.C.A. Radio Telegrams to "friends at sea," another routing first-class passengers to their special gangway. The State Department of Transportation has marked these piers for demolition. The ever present threat of fire may turn into a quicker, more merciful, and more spectacular solution.

The Chelsea docks were built at the turn of the century, the first of the 800-foot long "finger piers" designed specifically for the increasing number of transatlantic luxury liners, each larger than the last. Just as they were completed, Britain was adding the finishing touches to the 790-foot long sisters, *Mauretania* and *Lusitania*. These were owned by the Cunard Line and were by far the largest and fastest passenger ships yet built, taking just six days per crossing. Horse-drawn cabs and carts far outnumbered mechanical conveyances when the twin liners arrived in 1907. The public was deeply impressed by the four huge stacks on each, painted in Cunard's orange-red and black. Most other ships had only one to three funnels.

As the *Mauretania* and *Lusitania* prospered, another generation of liners followed that were bigger still, and lavish beyond expectation. The 800-foot-long *Olympic* arrived in 1911, featuring the first indoor swimming pool ever to go to sea. The *France* appeared a year later with a first-class restaurant done in Louis XIV decor, a room majestically set off by a sweeping grand staircase. The *Aquitania*—first to exceed 900 feet in length—had decorative touches of Tudor, Baroque, and Palladian. These queens of the Atlantic all used the Chelsea docks. Sometimes, in the afternoons, one could see as many as sixteen stacks, as four liners were prepared to sail on the evening tide. Thousands were employed cleaning and servicing the vessels, loading the fuel, provisions, and baggage for the next crossing. It made a colorful scene, full of bustle, promise, and excitement.

Occasionally a menacing note intruded. The *Titanic* was scheduled to arrive at the Chelsea piers on April 16, 1912, at the conclusion of her maiden voyage. On April 14, however, the "unsinkable" ship struck an iceberg and sank, with the loss of fifteen hundred lives. The Cunard liner *Carpathia* used the same dock to land some of the survivors. In May 1915, the *Lusitania* departed from the 14th Street pier on her regular run to England. A Ger-

Cunard's superb *Mauretania,* shown berthed at Pier 54 in Manhattan, held the transatlantic Blue Ribbon for twenty-two years, from 1907 until 1929. Another Cunarder, the *Samaria,* is to the left.

man U-boat torpedoed her off the coast of Ireland, and mobilized public opinion in support of America's entry into World War I.

For the duration of the war, the Chelsea piers, like the docks in great harbors everywhere, were busy participants in the war effort. As the twenties unfolded, however, and "normalcy" returned, Chelsea welcomed a new flotilla of liners, the *Paris,* the *Leviathan,* the *Majestic,* and the *Berengaria,* among others. Celebrities flocked to the Chelsea piers to be photographed and interviewed, leaving for, or returning from, Europe in high style.

In the summer of 1927, a ship put into Pier 57 that was to change the style of liners forever. She was the *Ile de France,* a tour de force of decorative splendor and stunning forerunner of the Art Deco. The interiors of earlier great ships had been based on shoreside themes: country houses, palaces, and historic concoctions. The *Ile de France* had a style that was invented just for her—"ocean liner style."

By 1933–34, the economic tide for the Chelsea-based fleet had changed. The Depression wreaked havoc and the Atlantic trade dropped from one million voyagers in 1929 to fewer than half as

Typical of the elegance during the *Mauretania*'s era on the North Atlantic is this view of part of the White Star Liner *Olympic*'s Main Lounge, circa 1911.

many within five years. Shipowners worried about their futures, and some vessels, like the ten-year-old *Minnetonka*, were sent to the scrap heap prematurely. Others, mostly bigger ships like the *Majestic* and *Berengaria*, were relegated to "booze cruises"—inexpensive, escapist jaunts along the American East Coast that side-stepped Prohibition and thus lured enough passengers to keep the liners running.

Traditional breakbulk freighter operations at Lower Manhattan's Pier 14. The Belgian Line's *Tervaete* served on the Congo run to Matadi and Boma.

The thirties, meanwhile, witnessed another quite different development at the Chelsea piers. Startling 1,000-footers like the *Normandie* and *Queen Mary* were steaming into port, signaling a mass migration by the bigger steamship firms to newly created, larger terminals in the West Fifties. "Luxury Liner Row" was born.

After a busy second World War Chelsea never regained its former importance for passenger shipping. A number of freighter firms rented space—bringing in goods from ports like Hamburg and Valparaiso, Yokohama and Glasgow. The era of the conventional freighter was on the wain by the middle sixties, however, giving way to large containerships, which required vast open pier spaces. By 1967, the last big tenants, the Grace and United States lines, relocated to Newark and Elizabeth in New Jersey. Chelsea's shipping days were over.

In 1974, the former Cunard world cruiseship *Caronia*, by then renamed *Caribia* and owned by rather questionable parties, was temporarily docked at Pier 56. She was an out-of-work, over-aged passenger ship totally obsolete in an age of zooming fuel costs and cheap junkets on charter airlines. Her inevitable destination was the scrapyards of Taiwan. Just before the final departure, however, her owners opened the ballrooms, staterooms, and corridors to a nostalgic public. Everything even remotely removable was price-tagged—from well-worn soft chairs in the Smoking Room to battered stainless steel cookware in the kitchens. Loyal fans of the great age of ocean liners walked off with cherished, and sometimes quite expensive, souvenirs—a telephone from a first-class suite, a panel of etched glass from the Lida Bar, a rather blistered deck chair. The old *Caronia* was stripped bare. As one of the last of the Atlantic Ocean notables, she was a final link to that marvelous series of floating palaces to which the Chelsea piers had formerly played host.

The Holland-America Line in Hoboken

In September 1980, a crane with one of those biting buckets leveled the last of the terminal buildings of the old Holland-America Line piers at the foot of Fifth Street in Hoboken. Although the piers themselves only dated from World War I, more than a century of history of one of the port's best known steamship firms seemed to disappear with those structures. While Holland-America still survives as a cruise company, it was a far different trade, in terms of ships, staff, and clientele, that those vanished piers witnessed. It was, in fact, another era, a class-conscious time, when liners mostly made port to port runs rather than the one-class luxury cruises that are the backbone of their business today. Imagine the scene as one of those three great ladies, the *Rotterdam*, the *Nieuw Amsterdam*, or the *Statendam* prepared to sail for Southampton, Le Havre, and finally Rotterdam. There were three classes of passengers, first, cabin, and tourist, ranging from business tycoons and Hollywood stars to college students heading for a budget summer on the Continent. I have vivid memories of such scenes from my youth in Hoboken during the fifties, when I grew up in the presence of those stately and magical Dutch queens.

On Fridays at noon, Hoboken would rattle from the throaty steam whistles of one of these three majestic ships. Moran tugs would be stationed at the bow. The hemp lines at the stern would

45

fall away first, and the aft end of the ship would begin slowly moving away from the pier. After another blast of the horns, the bow lines would be released from their bollards to fall into the Hudson and then be smartly pulled aboard ship. The liner was now free of the land. Gradually, she would begin to move away from the dockside. Then suddenly, the tug at the front end would change position, aiming directly into that towering gray hull. The ship would begin moving out, in reverse. Three long blasts on the whistles would cover the run into mid-river. At the pier's second level, family and friends would be cheering and waving. Often, they would release a cascade of wonderfully colored streamers fluttering down past the lower cargo doors to the water. In the Hudson, the sleek liner was now being swung with its bow pointed southward, toward the Lower Bay and ultimately the open Atlantic. Other ships, from the upper Manhattan piers, which would have sailed a half-hour earlier, would now be reaching the same point just off the Fifth Street pier. I can remember often watching breathlessly as one of the French or Greek liners would just squeeze past the Dutch ship while she was still in the last holding position, secured to the tugs for those final moments before being set free.

The wellwishers on the piers would begin to disappear from the cargo doors, leaving only the tangled lot of streamers. Stevedores would begin to shut the pier doors and soon they, too, would fade away. Silence would take over the empty berth. On the other side of the dock, just peering over the rooftop, another Holland-America liner—usually a smaller one like the *Maasdam* or *Noordam*—would be quietly loading for a Saturday sailing.

The beloved *Nieuw Amsterdam*, a ship that had a certain something—that blend of chic, comfort, and timelessness—that made her one of the most popular and favored liners on the transatlantic run, epitomized the Holland-America motto: "It's good to be on a well run ship!" Hundreds of thousands agreed, loving the great soft chairs in the wood-paneled Smoking Room, the two-story atmosphere of the main restaurant (inspired by the 1939 World's Fair), and those extra touches like the miniature brass mermaids that served as door handles in one of the bars.

The *Nieuw Amsterdam* had sailed out of the depths of the Depression as the biggest liner ever built in Holland—nearly 37,000 tons and 758 feet in length—and as the latest word in nautical design. She had been in service little more than a year when war erupted in the fall of 1939. Since she couldn't return to her

The magnificent *Nieuw Amsterdam*, flagship of the Holland-America Line, berthed at the foot of Fifth Street in Hoboken during the early fifties.

home waters, she was diverted to Caribbean cruising for those Americans who were still ignoring the bleak clouds on the horizon. When Holland finally did fall in the following spring, the liner broke off her two-week cruise off Venezuela and sped back to Hoboken. Her mission, now, was military work.

As one of the world's great troop carriers, she established an enviable record. She transported 378,361 military personnel on worldwide sailings that totaled over 530,000 miles—the equivalent of twenty-one times around the world. In so doing, she achieved some impressive averages. Her forty-four wartime voyages averaged 12,056 miles apiece. On each of them, she carried an average of 8,599 passengers, seven times her normal peacetime payload. Her gallant service attracted the favorable attention of Dutch royalty. In May 1944, Crown Princess Juliana, who later became Queen of the Netherlands, came aboard at Hoboken to attend a buffet luncheon in honor of the ship's heroic staff.

When hostilities ended, the *Nieuw Amsterdam* was refitted and returned to all her former glory. She resumed commercial service in October 1947, with Katharine Hepburn and Spencer Tracy among those on board for the first trip.

The 24,000-ton *Statendam* first arrived at Hoboken early in 1957. Due to a tugboat strike, she was denied the escort, up the river, of a festive flotilla of tugs. Her arrival, however, served to underscore the Dutch tradition of great seamanship. Her captain ordered some of his crew into lifeboats, and launched them into the icy waters of the Hudson. From their vantage points at water level, these mariners signaled to observers leaning over the rails, on board. They in turn relayed the signals to the bridge, and the great ship was carefully berthed without incident.

The *Statendam* was a beautifully appointed and well received liner. Her layout, however, hinted at the future of the Atlantic passenger trade. Instead of having the traditional three classes of passengers, as in the *Nieuw Amsterdam*, she had a mere eighty-four in first class, but nearly nine hundred in the tourist section. First class had been sharply reduced, and cabin class had disappeared entirely. The fabled North Atlantic rich, who once strolled along upper promenades and paraded into private grill rooms, were increasingly being diverted to speedy aircraft. Fortunately, however, there were still tourists in sizable numbers who preferred sea travel. Holland-America, like others, was suitably encouraged and finally agreed upon yet another major ship, the largest ever under Dutch colors, the 38,000-ton *Rotterdam*.

This latest flagship crossed to Hoboken in the late summer of

1959, with Crown Princess Beatrix, Juliana's daughter, on board to heighten the occasion. The *Rotterdam* was a ship of state, a glorious floating palace of art and design that admirably represented modern Holland. Even her profile was futuristic, replacing the conventional stack with twin side-by-side uptakes that were placed aft. Furthermore, she was adaptable for considerable one-class cruising. For just as the first-class voyagers had declined, so too the Atlantic route could no longer support such major ships in the bleak winter months (November through March). Soon, all of the Holland-America liners began to cruise—to the West Indies, the Mediterranean, and on one annual luxurious trip around the world. Even more change was still in the wind.

Four years after her maiden arrival on the Jersey side, the *Rotterdam* was towed across the Hudson, to Pier 40, at the foot of West Houston Street, then in the earliest stages of construction. It was the city's newest passenger ship terminal and certainly the most modern in the world at the time, with center-core and roof-top parking, drive-alongside privileges, and three full sides for berthing ships, each side about 800 feet long. Holland-America was offered the facility and could hardly refuse, especially considering the convenient access to midtown New York.

The transfer to the new pier did not come until 1963, but those final years at Hoboken left indelible impressions with me. There were those cold winter nights, when the extraordinary stillness was interrupted by the 10:00 P.M. departure whistles of one of the ships going off to the Caribbean. There were the quiet Sunday afternoons when many of the townspeople, taking the air, wandered to the pier to watch one of the liners tie up. There were, also, the Thursday night, six-hour charity cruises. Dozens of limousines, bearing the wealthy, powerful, and famous, would roll into Hoboken, escorted by cordons of motorcycle police. Their occupants, which could include the Eisenhowers, the Duke and Duchess of Windsor, Marlene Dietrich, and a host of celebrities from stage, screen, and television, would board a Holland-America liner, which would cruise down the river and out beyond the three-mile limit for gambling and a gala party. The society sections of the weekend newspapers were often filled with photos of celebrities taken during those floating festivities.

When Holland-America finally moved over to Pier 40, a small Portuguese freighter company rented the Fifth Street pier space, but life seemed never to be the same again. A few years later, they too moved elsewhere and the piers began to suffer a series of ruinous fires. They were turned into twisted, scorched masses of steel and debris. All that remains of these once busy docks is a crumbling inner bulkhead.

Hoboken's Pier B

"We were all given the day off from school and handed little American flags, and then told to go to River Street (adjacent to the docks) and wait for President Wilson to arrive." So recalled Erwin Abele, then a youngster of nine, who had come with his family from their native Sweden. He spent a good portion of his early life in Hoboken. The year was 1919 and President Woodrow Wilson was returning from France aboard the liner *George Washington*, following the historic Versailles Peace Treaty. The American ship docked at the Third Street pier in Hoboken, known in more recent years as Pier B.

The pier dates from just after the turn of the century. It was one of the four long finger piers built following the devastating Hoboken Pier Fire of 1900, in which over three hundred lives were lost, both ashore and afloat. One liner was completely burnt out and at least three others were seriously damaged. There was also great loss of adjacent waterfront properties. The chief tenants at the time were two German steamship giants, the Hamburg-America Line and the North German Lloyd, who, combined, possessed a fleet second only to that of Britain. So influential was the German presence, both socially and economically, that Hoboken was often thought of as a "suburb of Bremen" or "little Germany." Local Irish laborers often lived in small, crowded, rooming houses under the watchful eyes of proper German matrons. Such firms as Keuffel & Esser, which specialized in the manufacture of slide rulers and telescopic lenses, prospered. By the turn of the century, many of the German residents, becoming increasingly affluent, began to move farther uptown, away from the dock areas.

The fire-damaged piers were demolished and rebuilt, and the German shipping lines remained. Passenger vessels landed thousands each week (not including those in steerage, who were unloaded into tenders and ferries in the outer harbor and sent to Ellis Island). Ironically, many of these German-flag liners bore American names, such as *President Lincoln*, *Cincinnati*, and *Amerika*. The theory of early sales managers in both Bremen and Hamburg was that, since the immigrants were the largest class carried and the most profitable (despite the fares being less than $25 per

Pier B is to the far left in this aerial view of the Hoboken waterfront in the early twenties. Two Holland-America liners, the *Veendam* and *Nieuw Amsterdam*, are docked to the right, at the Company's Fifth Street berth.

51

person), American, or at least American-sounding, names would have the greatest appeal. In those days, immigrants frequently believed that if they traveled on a ship with an American name, it would simplify their entry and naturalization processes.

The Third Street pier welcomed the biggest liner in the world in 1913, the *Imperator* of the Hamburg-America Line. She was over 52,000 tons, 919 feet in length. She carried a staggering 4,594 passengers, 908 of whom traveled in opulent first class, and 1,772 in spartan steerage. There were 1,180 crew members, space for 8,500 tons of coal (oil did not come into use for ship propulsion until the early twenties), eighty-three lifeboats, and two motor launches. In spite of her size and impressive technology, the German days of glory were soon to come to an end with the onset of World War I.

Numerous ships that sailed under the German flag were at first laid up and then seized nine days after the United States entered the war in 1917. This group even included the brand new flagship of the Kaiser's merchant marine, the 56,000-ton *Vaterland*. The piers and neighboring property were also seized from the Germans by the Federal Government. Police forces from outside Hoboken were brought in to watch over the sites and even to close German shops near the docks. The area became "The Port of Embarkation" for the American Expeditionary Forces, the famed "doughboys." A small commemorative stone with a bronze plaque still stands beside River Street, in front of Pier B, to mark this important period in the history of Hoboken.

Transports, many of them ex-German liners, began sailing with large numbers of servicemen bound for the trenches of Europe. The process, however, was not without its problems. First, the existing 237 Hoboken saloons were a fierce temptation to the pier guards and troopship crews. Rather quickly, they were closed by official order, and remained so for the duration of the war. Christmas boxes posed another dilemma. The Government had suggested that it would be a nice gesture for the troops overseas to receive a present from home during Christmas 1917. Every box, however, had to be inspected—for bombs and other sinister contents—before it could be sent overseas. At first, the local command posted six officers and 250 men to inspection duty. Within days, the arrival rate of packages grew to such an extent that seventy officers and 1,160 men were needed.

At war's end, shoreside crews cheered each homecoming troopship as well as the transport trains that traveled away from the waterfront. There were, also, occasions of silence and tears,

The bow of the *Imperator* is aimed for the Lower Bay and the open Atlantic. In Manhattan the skyline is dominated by the 60-story Woolworth Building.

as other trains passed out of the docks with the wounded and the dead. Slowly thereafter, the piers returned to the normalcy of the twenties. The German occupants were gone, however, replaced by the likes of Cunard and the United States and Red Star Lines.

The legendary liner *Leviathan*, the former German *Vaterland*, had been seized during the war. She first sailed under Yankee colors as a troopship, and later as a luxury liner. In 1934 she was tied up at the Third Street pier, a victim of the Depression. There she sat, idle, for nearly four years, turning the south side of the pier into a lay-up berth. Her red, white and blue funnels faded in the summer suns, her lifeboats were stripped off, her innards rattled in darkness and a handful of watchmen looked after what was once the largest liner afloat. She had grown old, too expensive to operate, and would have required costly repairs and upgrading. There was little hope. In the end, a small armada of tugs

In the twenties and thirties especially, when superliners like the *Leviathan* were about to sail, thousands went to the dockside.

yanked her from her Hoboken slip on a cold January afternoon in 1938. Belching thick black smoke, she set course for Scotland to be junked.

The Hoboken piers contributed to another world conflict, although far more with munitions and cargo than troops. In the late forties, they were selected by the Port Authority for redevelopment. Three of the original piers were demolished, leaving the Third Street pier, renamed Pier B, as the sole survivor of the earlier era. The American Export Lines became the major tenant and remained so until 1970. A variety of foreign-flag companies followed until the last freighter, a vessel out of Bombay, departed in 1978. The three piers were among the last deep-sea ship terminals still in use along the Hudson. The vast container facilities of Port Newark and Elizabeth, farther west in Jersey, were now the main centers of the port's ocean shipping.

After a brief stint of idleness, Pier B burst into flames on a windy November day in 1980, spilling a huge blanket of smoke across the Hudson and onto mid-Manhattan. The fire persisted for several days and spelled the end for the last of the old German liner piers in Hoboken. It is now scheduled to be demolished.

Among the last ships to use Hoboken's historic Pier B were the American Export Freighters. Here the *Export Builder* is returning from a voyage to the Mediterranean.

IV THE URBAN ARCHIPELAGO
F.J.D.

IT WAS A STORY that, as a child, I had heard many times from my mother: how she had come from Ireland on a ship and landed on Ellis Island, in New York Harbor. When she had a physical examination it was discovererd she had chicken pox, and she was taken off the island on a small boat. She feared that they were taking her back to Ireland and her dream of coming to the United States was ended.

The boat did not take my mother back to Ireland but up the East River to another island, North Brother Island. There she was placed in a communicable disease hospital, under quarantine, until the chicken pox passed and she was allowed to enter the United States.

This story made an indelible impression on my mind, and from it I developed an insatiable interest in the lesser known islands of the port. Over the years, I have researched these islands, have talked to people who had worked on them, and have even had the opportunity to visit some of them.

Sailing into the Port of New York and New Jersey, either from the main sea route by the Ambrose Channel from the Atlantic Ocean, or through the back door entrance of Long Island Sound, it becomes evident that this is not a typical seacoast city, but a group of islands that cluster together to form one of the finest, best-protected, natural harbors in the world.

Early in the port's history, Manhattan, the most important island in the group, became a Dutch settlement, followed by Staten Island and Long Island, as the population grew. The major islands were soon joined together with the mainland and to each other by a great transportation web. First there were ferryboats, and later, great bridges and tunnels. Today few New York citizens are aware of the fact that they live and work on islands.

Four of the five boroughs that make up the City of New York are located on islands, with only the Bronx totally part of the mainland of the United States. Oddly enough, part of Manhattan

Above: Hoffman, one of the port's man-made islands. It was built as a quarantine hospital site and later used as a maritime training school during World War II, but is now deserted, although part of Gateway National Park. *Below:* Swinburne Island was once used for a crematory in conjunction with the hospital on nearby Hoffman Island. The buildings are left over from World War II when the island was used for one end of an anchorage for a submarine net that protected the harbor.

started out as part of the island, but when the Harlem Ship Canal was cut, the remaining peninsula was joined to the mainland by the filling in of the Spuyten Duyvil Creek, so that today it is technically part of the continent. A recent court decision completed the matter by making the section part of Manhattan but not part of New York County, so residents of Marble Hill have Bronx zip codes and telephone numbers and vote for officials in the Bronx.

Over the years the various islands that make up this archipelago have grown with landfill, have been joined to other islands and the mainland, or have even been dredged out of existence. Of the fifty-odd islands that make up the city, many are still outside the pale, mostly unused, forgotten lands, all with long interesting histories, but uncertain futures. The information that follows is about these strange lands.

Hoffman and Swinburne Islands

Coming in by ship from the Atlantic Ocean to the harbor, the first small islands that one sees off the shores of Staten Island on the port side are Hoffman and Swinburne. Prior to 1872, Orchard Shoals was just one of the many shallow areas in the port; the two and a half acre Swinburne and the eleven and a quarter acre Hoffman islands are man-made. They took six years to build and cost some $300,000, a good part of which may have been absorbed by William Marcy Tweed, who was, in his day, a political power not exactly known for putting the public's interest first.

In the days before the discoveries of Dr. Walter Reed, summer in New York City always spelled deaths from yellow fever. So great was the fear of the disease that local citizens kept burning down quarantine hospitals on Staten Island, until officials found the only solution was to move the hospitals out into the harbor, onto Hoffman and Swinburne islands. Hoffman, a mere eight feet above sea level, housed the main hospital, or pesthouse, while Swinburne contained a crematory for the many who died. Both islands protected the nation against pestilence and plague until their functions were taken over by a new hospital at the Immigration Station on Ellis Island.

The military used the islands in both World Wars, and one end of a submarine net protecting the harbor was anchored on Hoffman Island. One of the first training stations for merchant seamen in World War II was located on the islands. This was the last major use they had. Today, both islands have joined others in the harbor as deserted, forgotten lands, with Hoffman being one of the main nesting grounds on the east coast for sea gulls. Both islands are now part of the Gateway National Park.

Lafayette Island

One of the many lost islands of the harbor is Lafayette. It was built as a fort to protect the port against the British during the War of 1812, along with many other fortified structures on other harbor islands. Located just two hundred yards off the Brooklyn shores, Fort Lafayette never fired a shot from any of its seventy-three guns, but did go on to serve the nation as a prison during the Civil War. In World War II, warships would unload their ammunition there before entering the inner harbor. Lafayette faded into history in 1964 when it became the base for the Brooklyn tower of the Verrazano Narrows Bridge that joins Staten Island and Brooklyn.

Liberty Island

The upper bay contains three islands of great historical interest that are fairly well known to the general public: Governors, Liberty, and Ellis Island. Of all the out-islands in the harbor none receives more attention and visitors than Liberty Island, with its Statue of Liberty and Museum of Immigration. Access to Liberty, which is a National Park, may only be made on a Circle Line ferry from Manhattan's Battery. The base of the Statue of Liberty was once Fort Wood, built, like Lafayette, for the War of 1812.

Governors Island

One of the first settlements in the harbor was on Governors Island, which the Dutch called Nut Island when they came over in 1632. This 170-acre island is one of the most beautiful and unspoiled places in the harbor, containing many eighteenth and nineteenth century houses and traffic-free paths and roads, bordered by trees and lawns. Fort Jay, built by citizen volunteers, is now used for housing, and Castle William still points some of its remaining guns, of the hundred it had, at lower Manhattan.

In 1664, the British came to Governors Island before taking

Fort Lafayette, off the Brooklyn shore, is one of the islands in the port that has disappeared. It is now the Brooklyn base for the tower of the Verrazano-Narrow Bridge, between Brooklyn and Staten Island.

the city from the Dutch, and the house built for the English governors in 1708, which gave the island its name, still stands. One of the most active islands, having been an Army garrison from the 1790s to 1966, when it became a U.S. Coast Guard base and training station, the island grew from seventy-two acres to its present size with fill taken from the first subway excavation in New York City at the turn of the century. Only people with official business are permitted on the ferry from the Battery, except for special tours, booked in advance with the Coast Guard.

Ellis Island

It is estimated that one-quarter to one-half of the present population of these United States can trace their ancestry back to relatives who passed through the "Golden Door" on Ellis Island. In Colonial days, before pollution of the harbor waters, both Ellis and Liberty islands were called Oyster Islands. Ellis is another island that grew from its original acreage to its present size with landfill—from 3.3 to 27.5 acres—some of which was said to be ballast from ships. Over the years since it passed from the Indians, it has had many uses: as Fort Gibson in the War of 1812; as a naval munitions depot; as a place to hang pirates, and from the

61

years 1892 to 1954, as the Plymouth Rock of New York Harbor, the legendary immigration station.

The island was reopened to the public in 1976, as a result of the efforts of the Ellis Island Restoration Commission. Until utilities are installed, it may only be visited from April to October. Access to Ellis Island is by the Circle Line ferry from the Battery and Liberty State Park in New Jersey. Its continued restoration now comes under the care of the Statue of Liberty-Ellis Island Foundation, and there are plans to build a temporary bridge to it from Liberty State Park.

Shooters, Pralls, and Island of the Meadows

There is no finer example of urban waterfront decay than Kill Van Kull and Arthur Kill's waterways, which extend from the upper bay to Raritan Bay, dividing New Jersey and Staten Island. These waterways are among the most important in the port, however, for they are the route of the large oil tankers and containerships that enable the port to maintain its number one position in the nation.

Of the three islands in this area, Shooters had been a shipyard from Colonial times. About sixty years ago, the yard closed

An Early Drawing of Ellis Island

and the owners just seemed to walk away, leaving a collection of flotsam and jetsam of dock, sunken tugs, and even drydocks. When the commercial maritime interests of the port asked the Army Corps of Engineers to remove the fifty-one acre island, to make it safer for the estimated three hundred vessels that pass it daily, it seemed like a good idea. The only claim to fame the island had in the course of its history was the fact that President Theodore Roosevelt once went there to christen the yacht *Meteor*, built for Kaiser Wilhelm II of Germany.

When the announcement was made of plans to blast the island off the map, at an estimated cost of $60 million, the environmentalists came out in force against it. It seems that Shooters Island, with all the derelict wooden vessels, pilings and piers, provides the perfect rookery for five species of herons. The birds enjoy the isolation of the island; it is practically impossible for visitors to land on it. Since there are few such nesting places left on the East Coast, the Audubon Society feels it may be the end of the herons if the island is removed. At present the new 950-foot long containerships of the United States Lines slowly pass dangerously close to the island, with only a few yards to spare.

Farther down the Arthur Kill waterway, just before the entrance to the Rahway River, is Pralls Island. Named after the family that once used it to grow hay, this barren island seems to have no real history. It was used after both World Wars as an anchorage for small surplus military boats, pending disposal. In 1984, the eighty-acre island became part of the New York City Parks Department, to be used only for a sanctuary for birds.

It's easy to find the Isle of Meadows: just follow the endless convoys of tugs with garbage scows sailing to the Fresh Kills landfill area. Soon this island will blend into the mainland of Staten Island when the scows have filled the area. It is hoped that the planned park will be an improvement over the natural wetlands it destroyed.

Jamaica Bay's Islands: Broad Channel, Barren

The largest concentration of islands in the port is in the Jamaica Bay area. Most of these are now part of the Gateway National Park, and a wildlife refuge for birds. John F. Kennedy Airport is located in this area, but in spite of the roar of the jets, there's still tranquillity on these deserted islands with their white sandy beaches.

During the Prohibition era, Jamaica Bay was a haven for rum-runners, and Broad Channel Island, now joined to Brooklyn and the Rockaway Peninsula by bridges, earned the name "Little Cuba." History was recently repeated when a large drug bust was made on a fishing boat in these same waters.

Barren Island, now part of Marine Park, was sold to the Dutch by the Canarsie Indians. It became a city dump and was the site of a glue factory, which got its raw material from the city's dead horses. A colony of hardy souls lived in the dump and were only displaced in 1939, when the park was built. Today Barren Island is headquarters for the Gateway National Park and the Brooklyn Air Station of the U.S. Coast Guard's helicopters.

U-Thant

U-Thant Island, formerly called Belmont Island, the name still found on most charts, is the first harbor island encountered in the East River going north from the Battery. It is located opposite the United Nations Building, off the southern tip of Roosevelt Island, which is one of the few islands to make the leap from prison, hospital, and decline into a "new town." When a tunnel was built for trolley cars under the East River, between Manhat-

U-Thant Island is just a speck in the East River, opposite the United Nation's complex. The island is man-made from the material excavated to build the IRT subway tunnel from Queens.

64

Mill Rock Island is in the East River at the entrance to Hell Gate Passage and was used as a fort site during the War of 1812. The explosives with which the rocks were cleared from Hell Gate were manufactured on this island to protect the city from possible damage.

tan and Queens, a shaft was sunk on Man-of-War reef and the excavated soil and rock were used to form what became Belmont Island, named for August Belmont, the builder of the original New York subway, and the man who finished the project. The tunnel was started by piano maker William Steinway and is still named for him. It never saw any trolley cars, but is still in use today as part of the IRT subway system. The name Belmont was changed to U-Thant to honor the late Secretary General of the United Nations, and today a peace arch has joined the small navigation day marker on the island.

Mill Rock Island

The Port of New York almost lost its number one position in the nation's seaports at the turn of the century, and except for the work of Army Engineers in clearing the rocks and reefs of Hell Gate in the East River, it would have. Opposite East 96th Street in Manhattan is Mill Rock, a small island that played a major part in this project. Once two small islands that were later

The above photo shows the massive hole dug to tunnel under the Hudson River in order to blast the rocks out of Hell Gate.

joined together during the War of 1812, Mill Rock had a block-house with cannons that waited for the British, who never came.

The Army Engineers used this island as a base to mix the explosives to blast Flood Rock out of the Hell Gate channel. This explosion was the largest made by man prior to the nuclear bomb. The Federal Government deeded Mill Rock Island to the city in 1958, and it appears on the map today as a park, although the only access is by boat, bucking a five-knot current. A recently released plan called for building a windmill on the island to generate electricity.

The Bay of the Brothers

After one passes through the maelstrom of the Hell Gate waters in the East River, two more deserted islands come into view, North Brother and South Brother. They are located in the Bay of the Brothers, between the Bronx and Queens, near Rikers Island, which is known for its city prison. The Dutch called these islands *Gesellen*, a word meaning "companions."

North Brother island, the larger of the two, is 20.5 acres and has a long history. It was the home of Typhoid Mary, who spent the remainder of her life there after it was determined that she was a carrier of the disease. In 1904, it was on this island that the excursion steamer *General Slocum* ran aground after catching fire in the Hell Gate passage. After World War II, the island became a home for returning veterans going to college in local universities. The last use for the buildings that are still standing, although heavily vandalized, was when Riverside Hospital was used to house narcotic addicts. There have been many plans to use the island, but it remains empty today.

One of the few privately owned islands in the harbor is South Brother, which, since 1958, has been the property of the Hampton Scows Co. Colonel Jacob Ruppert, who made his money brewing beer on the East Side of Manhattan and owned the New York Yankees ball club, built a summer house on the island in 1894. His house, which burned down in 1907, was the last structure to occupy the land. The only visitors now are prisoners trying to escape from the nearby prison on Rikers Island. Most of them are quickly picked up by the Harbor Police.

Above: Aerial photo of North Brother Island, off the Bronx shore, one of the many deserted islands in the waters around New York City, and for years the home of "Typhoid Mary." *Below:* South Brother Island, once privately owned, has a much less colorful history than that of North Brother Island, an edge of which can be seen, upper left.

Hart Island

The last of the semi-deserted islands within the city is Hart Island, located off the east side of City Island, in the Bronx. The history of Hart follows the pattern of many of the others: use by the military, and use as a place to hide less fortunate members of society. Over the years since it was bought from private owners in 1869, it has been used as a quarantine hospital, workhouse for paupers, home for skid-row citizens, disciplinary barracks for the U.S. Navy in World War II, a Nike missile base (which like the many other forts built on harbor islands for the War of 1812, has never fired a shot at any enemy), and until 1976, as the Phoenix House for drug addicts. Civil War Union soldiers were buried there, but veterans organizations thought so little of the island that they had the bodies removed to a national cemetery in 1941.

Hart Island still has one prime use as a potter's field for the city's unclaimed dead. Forty-eight prisoners live on the island, in portable housing, and bury the dead that come from the city morgue. A ferryboat, *Michael Cosgrove*, makes the short trip from City Island to Hart Island. A large monument with a cross dominates the northern end of the island where the graves are located.

All the islands seem to have had great plans for a future that never materialized. A black developer, Solomon Riley, once

Hart Island, Long Island Sound

planned a "Negro Coney Island," on Hart Island. A 1972 study outlined a Monte Carlo, or Riviera complex. New York State thought Hart was an ideal location for a fossil fuel generating station. Today the stone seawall, built by long-forgotten prisoners, circles the graves of more than seven hundred thousand penniless, nameless souls.

The Islands' Future

Why, in a city with such a large population, and some of the highest land values, are there so many acres of unused land on the harbor islands? Recently, the new town on Roosevelt Island has proven the advantage and popularity of island housing. The main problem seems to be the cost of the ferry service for these islands outside the transportation loops.

Many planners feel that the harbor islands comprise a land bank for future needs of the city. Perhaps the cost of development and round-the-clock ferry service, or a bridge where possible, will some day be offset by demands for the land. For the present, the deserted islands will remain just names on a navigation chart, of interest to few. They are shrouded in the mists of history and have uncertain futures.

V GREAT LADIES OF THE HIGH SEAS   W.H.M.

The Lusitania and Mauretania

The world's greatest and grandest ocean liners, which sailed from such ports as Liverpool and Southampton, Le Havre, Rotterdam, Hamburg, and Genoa, were intended to serve only one port on the Western end of the Atlantic passage: New York. These ships, with as many as four funnels, lined the finger piers of New York harbor (both in Manhattan and across the river, in Hoboken) in an age well before the development of aircraft. They were the marvels of their time—brilliant in decor, design, engineering, and technology. They were "the floating cities," the largest moving objects made by man. Some of the most notable developments in ocean transportation came soon after the turn of the century, spurred, no doubt, by the endless and increasing stream of immigrants, traveling in steerage. By 1907, twelve thousand were arriving in New York every day. The pace of travel was also picking up, and a battle, of sorts, for prestige and honor was joined between Imperial Britain and Imperial Germany. Ocean liners were the weapons.

Beginning in 1897, the powerful German shippers, namely the Hamburg American Line and the North German Lloyd, began to turn out a series of large, very powerful, four-funnel ships that were called the first of the "superliners." Soon the status symbol of four funnels conjured up only the biggest and safest ships, and therefore the most popular, especially in the minds of the immigrants who furnished the lucrative steerage trade. These German ships snatched the most prized honors (for world's fastest and world's largest ships) from the smug British. They were the 14,300-ton *Kaiser Wilhelm der Grosse* (1897), the 16,500-ton *Deutschland* (1900), the 14,900-ton *Kronprinz Wilhelm* (1901), the 19,300-ton *Kaiser Wilhelm II* (1903) and, the last of this early group, the 19,300-ton *Kronprinzessin Cecilie* (1906). These "German mons-

ters,'' as the British called them, had to be challenged and surpassed. Shipping ministers in London approached the Cunard
Company of Liverpool, and offered not only a sizable construction loan, but also special operating subsidies for a pair of British
superliners. They became the *Lusitania* and *Mauretania* of 1907,
two of the best-known passenger ships ever built.

The *Lusitania* arrived first, in September 1907, to great ac-
claim, and seized all the honors from the earlier German vessels.
She is, however, best remembered for her tragic demise, having
been torpedoed and sunk by a German U-boat off the Irish Coast,
on May 7, 1915. Eleven hundred and ninety-eight people, including one hundred twenty-four Americans, perished in a disaster that, more than any other, brought the United States into
the first World War. The *Mauretania*, on the other hand, which
was commissioned two months later, in November 1907, had a
highly popular, profitable, and successful career. She was one of
the greatest of the great liners, and held the Blue Ribbon for speed
for twenty-two years, until 1929.

The *Mauretania* (790 feet long, and weighing in at almost
32,000 tons) and her sister liner were also technologically inno-
vative. They were the first major ships to be propelled by steam
turbine power rather than by the old steam triple-expansion
method. This allowed for a much cleaner, faster operation. Below
deck, the *Mauretania* boasted 25 boilers and 192 furnaces. These
were fed coal at the rate of 1,000 tons a day from her storage hold
containing in excess of 6,000 tons. Making Liverpool in six days,
from her West Fourteenth Street berth, the new Cunarder ran at
an unparalleled 25 knots. She was the beginning of Britain's new
golden age of passenger shipping. In quick time, larger liners were
on the drawing boards, including the sisterships *Olympic* and *Titanic* of 1911–1912, for the White Star Line—which were for the
run out of Southampton—and then for an even larger Cunarder,
the *Aquitania* of 1914.

On board, the style of one's surroundings varied directly with
one's affluence. First-class passengers, cosseted by maids and
cabin servants, were transported in unparalleled luxury. The decor was that of a fabulous English manor house, complete with
marble columns, crystal chandeliers, working fireplaces, stained-
glass skylights, and even a potted-palm court. Less wealthy travelers put up with less gracious conditions. The immigrants, in the
infamous steerage, consisted of the largest number of passengers,
carried in the smallest amount of space. Of the nearly one thousand crew members, the most deserving of pity were the two

hundred stokers, "the black gangs," who fed coal into the ever-hungry boilers under inferno-like conditions.

The passenger run between Liverpool and New York was, like most others, interrupted in that tense summer of 1914. War broke out in Europe and the *Mauretania* was sent on an irregular run to Halifax. Later, as the political situation grew far more serious, all commercial service ceased, and the liner was painted over in drab wartime grays. Early in the following year, she made three round trips, as a troopship, to Gallipoli. Then, in a sudden swing of official direction, she was outfitted as a hospital ship and re-painted in white, with huge red crosses along her sides. With other vessels, she made a heroic voyage from the battlefields of the Mediterranean home to Britain with 6,298 wounded aboard.

In 1916, she was transferred back to troop service and began to reappear on the North Atlantic, sailing out of New York. For this duty, years before radar was developed, she was disguised in "dazzle paint," a clever system of geometric shapes of various shades of gray that enabled her to blend with the sea and escape the sinister U-boats. To the American doughboys who later sailed aboard her, she was affectionately known as the "Maury."

In 1919, the *Mauretania* was restored for peacetime sailings, trading out of Southampton, however, instead of Liverpool. She became a member of Cunard's "Big Three"—their weekly Atlantic express trio. The *Berengaria* was the flagship; the *Aquitania* was thought to be the most beautiful; and the *Mauretania* was still the world's fastest. The postwar era had changed the transatlantic trade. The American quota system was established in 1921, and vastly curtailed the once-lucrative steerage business. New, more refined, tourist-class sections had to be created instead. Further-more, fuel oil came into its own and soon replaced the old coal systems. In the early twenties, the long-suffering stokers were fast disappearing from the world's major liners.

The *Mauretania* was appropriately converted and improved during an extended refit in 1921. Life on board during the twen-ties reflected the times. Silent film stars were photographed along her decks, ten-course suppers were enjoyed in the first-class res-taurant, and during the bleak winters, three hundred millionaires were attended by her eight hundred staff members during idyllic, six-week, Mediterranean cruises. Although well into middle age, for a ship, the *Mauretania* remained one of the most popular ves-sels afloat. But a new breed of faster and larger ships was taking shape on the drawing boards. Even Cunard was looking ahead to a twin-liner express run for two enormous ships that would become the illustrious *Queen Mary* (1936) and *Queen Elizabeth* (1940).

In the summer of 1929, the *Mauretania*'s old speed record, which had stood for so many years, was topped by the 51,000-ton *Bremen*. This German successor was a sleek, almost flat-topped vessel that averaged 27.92 knots for the crossing, against the old Cunarder's 27.22 knots. In the race, there were, allegedly, valiant efforts by the *Mauretania*'s loyal crew, which included tossing some furniture into the furnaces in the hopes of raising additional steam. The new German persevered, however, and congratulations were flashed from the *Mauretania*'s bridge.

Once the Depression set in, the Atlantic passenger trade began to dwindle—from over a million voyagers in 1930 to less than half that number by 1935. Soon afterward, the aged *Mauretania* was sent on one-class cruises, to tropic ports like Nassau, Havana, and Kingston, and occasionally on longer trips to the Mediterranean. She seemed demoted, even running $10 overnight trips to "nowhere." She was, in fact, struggling for her very existence. As passengers became less plentiful, the older ships were retired first. The *Mauretania* left New York for the last time in September 1934, on the same day that her successor, the far larger and faster *Queen Mary*, was being launched in Scotland.

The *Mauretania* might have been the ideal candidate for conversion to a museum, a testament to the gilded age of the ocean liner, but the economics of the time were a problem. Rusted and stripped, and with many of her luxurious fittings auctioned-off, one of the greatest liners of all went off to the scrapyards of Rosyth, in Scotland.*

The Ile de France

The *Ile de France* was the first large liner to be built after World War I. Her owners, the French Line, predicted that she would be the most magnificent ship of her time. She was not intended to be either the biggest or the fastest—or, in fact, statistically notable in any way. Her brilliance was due to her interiors. They were revolutionary, totally modern, and in sharpest contrast to all previous liners.

---

*A second *Mauretania* was added by Cunard in 1939, and continued in service until 1965, but she never had quite the magical success and popularity of her predecessor.

Built at France's St. Nazaire shipyards, she was launched on March 14, 1926, in the presence of thousands of officials, workers, and guests. She was second of a quartet of French liners, each one larger and grander than the last. The *Paris* of 1921 had been the first, the *Lafayette* of 1930, was the third, and the *Champlain* of 1932, the fourth.

When the press first visited the new *Ile de France* in the late spring of 1927, they were quick to write glowingly of her accommodations and their novelty. The 390 first-class staterooms were done in as many different decorative styles and prompted one appraiser to assert that "the *Ile de France* was more eclectic than modern." Overall, she heralded the modern age of ocean greyhound, with angular furniture, sweeping columns, glass panels, high-gloss floors, indirect lighting, and a prevailing sense of spaciousness. The bar was acclaimed as the longest afloat, a feature that appealed enormously to thirsty Americans, who formed the majority of her clientele, and who were suffering the agonies of Prohibition. The main restaurant, also hailed at the time as the largest ever to go to sea, rose three decks in height and had a spectacular staircase as an entrance. The cuisine made the *Ile de*

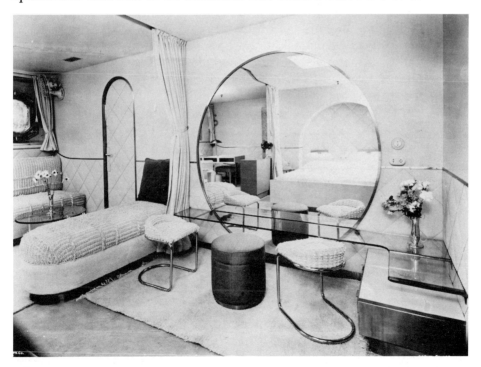

Sumptuous living on a liner of the 1930s: the Surinam Suite aboard the *Nieuw Amsterdam*.

France's passengers the best-fed on the North Atlantic. The grand foyer was four decks high, and the chapel was done in Gothic with fourteen pillars. There were even a shooting gallery, a merry-go-round, and a fully-equipped gymnasium.

Accommodations were arranged as follows: 670 in first class, 408 in cabin class, and 508 in third class. All of the cabins, including those for third class, had beds instead of the customary bunks. First class offered a large assortment of suites and *"cabins deluxe."* These were praised as the finest offering of their kind. By 1935, the *Ile de France* had carried more first-class passengers than any other transatlantic liner. She was described as "the cheeriest way to cross the North Atlantic" and as "a bit of mainland France, herself."

At the outbreak of World War II, in September, 1939, the *Ile de France* was at Pier 88, at the foot of West 48th Street, just across from the great *Normandie* and Cunard's *Queen Mary.* Fearing enemy advances, the French Line, like so many others, had no wish to send their ships to the homeland. As the *Ile de France* was occupying an important high-traffic berth, she was towed, by ten tugboats, to Staten Island, where she was laid up. Her normal staff of eight hundred was reduced to one hundred. Months later, in March, she was put on loan to the British Admiralty and, on May 1, was despatched to Europe, and then to far-off Singapore, with war materials. Several uncrated bombers were even stowed on her aft decks. Once in the East, she was formally seized by the British, following the fall of France.

The gray-painted troopship, *Ile de France,* returned to New York in the autumn of 1941, and was sent to the Todd Shipyards in Brooklyn's Erie Basin. During a 120-day conversion and overhaul, she was given berths for 9,706 servicemen compared to 1,486 peacetime passengers. Her kitchens were modernized; her machinery was thoroughly refitted; her entire plumbing system was scrapped and replaced. Soon afterward, the *Ile de France* went back to transporting troops for the British Government, serving again in Eastern waters. She sailed under two flags, Britain and Free France, one of very few ships to sail under dual flags during wartime.

Based at Saigon and later at Bombay, her frequent wartime partners were two comparable liners, the Dutch *Nieuw Amsterdam* and Cunard's second *Mauretania.* Often, they sailed on the Capetown to Suez troop shuttle. Then, in 1943, the *Ile de France* was returned to the North Atlantic, under Cunard management, and paired with another exiled French liner, the *Pasteur.*

The *Ile de France* was officially decommissioned by the British in September, 1945. There was little time for repairs or restoration, however. She was hurriedly placed on "austerity service" to Canada, to New York, and to troubled French Indochina. It was not until the spring of 1947 that she was returned to the French Line and sent to St. Nazaire yards for rebuilding. The task took over two years. Her third, "dummy," funnel came off, and two, new, streamlined stacks were fitted in place of the other pair. Her accommodations were modernized to a more contemporary configuration: 541 in first class, 577 in cabin class, and 227 in tourist class. She left Le Havre on July 21, 1949, on her first post-war commercial crossing to New York. Fireboats, tugs, and harbor craft gave her a glorious reception as befitted her "second maiden voyage." A year later, the 44,000-ton *Ile de France* was joined by the even larger 51,000-ton *Liberte*, which had started life, before the war, as the German *Europa*, but was totally renovated and recommissioned as flagship of the French Line.

Dressed in wartime grey, the troopship *Ile de France* is shown in 1945 at the Todd Shipyards in Hoboken.

The *Ile de France* made the headlines in New York on several occasions in the remaining years of her life. In July 1956, while outbound for Europe, she rescued 753 survivors from the sinking Italian liner, *Andrea Doria,* off Nantucket. In October of that same year, she was lashed by a violent Atlantic storm, which flooded six of her passenger cabins and dented the superstructure. In February 1957, she went aground during a Caribbean cruise, at Fort de France, Martinique. The damage was extensive. Her passengers had to leave the ship and be flown home, while an ocean-going tug was summoned to tow the liner to Newport News, Virginia, the nearest drydock capable of handling the 791-foot long ship.

The *Ile de France* attained her thirty-first birthday in 1958. That same year, aircraft began siphoning off transatlantic passenger traffic. Her former first-class roster of celebrities had disappeared, her wintertime crossings had dwindled, and the problems of old age had beset her. Regretfully, the French faced the obvious: the beloved *Ile de France* must be retired. She left New York that November on her last crossing. Laid up at Le Havre, she sparked a number of rumors concerning her eventual fate. One group proposed her as a museum ship, while another proposed her as a hotel and gambling casino along the Riviera. The Sheraton Hotel firm allegedly considered her as a resort ship based on Martinique. The most elaborate scheme, coming from loyalist fans, was to cut her masts, funnels, and superstructure for bridge clearance, and sail her along the Seine, into the heart of Paris. In reality, the French Line was quite pleased when the most serious bid came from Japanese scrappers, thereby allowing the ship a quiet, dignified ending in some faraway harbor.

Thousands lined the docksides at Le Havre, in February 1959, as the *Ile de France* sailed off to Osaka. Under the command of a small Japanese crew, she hoisted Japanese colors once at sea and was renamed the *Furansu (France) Maru.* Near the end of this last voyage, the Japanese suddenly leased the ship to a Hollywood film company, for $4,000 a day. She was to be used as a big prop in the production of "The Last Voyage," a fictional tale of the last passage of a famed transpacific liner. The French were horrified that their beloved ship would be subjected to such indignities. The film crews planned to use explosives, to gut some of her interiors, and to deliberately allow the forward funnel to collapse on the wheelhouse. Even the watertight compartments were partly flooded. The French went to court and at least succeeded in having her French Line funnels repainted.

After several weeks in the Inland Sea, the *Ile de France* was returned to Osaka and scrapped. To many maritime historians, she is one of the transatlantic immortals, that group of extraordinary liners that will live in memory along with her: the first *Mauretania*, the *Titanic*, the *Normandie*, and the *Queen Mary*.

The Normandie

The early thirties was the peak of ocean liner competition. Despite the havoc of the Depression, the world's biggest and most beautiful ships were delivered in these bleak years. In spite of a greatly diminished trade, they were important as floating statements of brilliance and goodwill. The Germans had their giant speed queens *Bremen* and *Europa*, from 1929 and 1930; the Italians had their first large team, the *Rex* and *Conte di Savoia* of 1932; and the British were looking ahead not only to the world's largest passengers liners, but the very fastest as well. These last named ships were, of course, the *Queen Mary* of 1936 and her running-mate, the *Queen Elizabeth* of 1940.

While the *Queen Mary* was being assembled in Scotland, the French were at work on their own supership at the St. Nazaire shipyards. She was the *Normandie*, the most sumptuous liner of all time. Although she sailed to New York for only four years, from 1935 until 1939, she left a glittering legend, unsurpassed to this day.

The 83,000-ton *Normandie*, the most luxurious superliner of all time, arriving off Lower Manhattan in 1936.

The *Normandie* was designed to achieve three ambitions for the French Line. She was to be the world's largest liner—and was the first ever to exceed 1,000 feet in length and 60,000 tons in weight. She was to be the fastest—and claimed the Blue Ribbon from Italy's *Rex*. Most significantly, she was to be a dazzling, floating demonstration of French art and technology. The *Queen Mary* was her only serious rival, and then only for size and speed. The French liner remained unchallenged in the beauty and innovation of her accommodations. Later, when the *Queen Mary* proved to be slightly larger than the *Normandie* the French sent their flagship into drydock and had an unneeded deckhouse added, which pushed her overall tonnage above the Cunarder's by some 2,000 tons.

In the scale and standard of her luxury and novelty, the *Normandie* could not be matched. The French Government put up much of the ship's $60 million cost, by far the largest amount ever paid for a liner at the time. This far exceeded the $36 million cost of the *Queen Mary*.

The *Normandie*'s keel was laid in November 1931. As the giant ship grew in size, the Paris offices of the French Line were overwhelmed with naming suggestions: *La Belle France, General Pershing, Jeanne D'Arc,* and even *Maurice Chevalier,* to list a few. Madame Lebrun, the First Lady of France, named the ship the *Normandie* during the launching ceremonies on October 29, 1932, as the still-unfinished hull slid into the Loire River, creating a roaring backwash.

Work on the *Normandie* had stopped during the depth of the Depression. When work finally resumed, it was announced that the maiden voyage from LeHavre to New York would be postponed until the spring of 1935. She finally crossed in May of that year. The interested public marveled at the new liner's raked silhouette with three large red-and-black funnels. The height of these diminished from fore to aft, and the rear stack was actually a ventilator and dog kennel disguised as a funnel. Outdoors, her upper decks were amazingly clear; not a ventilator, deckhouse, or chain locker marred the picture. All of the technical needs were hidden with great care below deck. The bow was sharply curved and clearly demonstrated the extent to which design affected speed and performance. But if her exterior was splendid, her interior was a marvel.

The *Normandie* was the most extravagantly decorated liner of all time. The main restaurant was done in hammered glass and bronze, with Lalique fixtures. It was slightly longer than the Hall

The first-class foyer aboard the *Normandie,* an example of Art Deco on the high seas.

of Mirrors at Versailles, rose three decks in height, and seated a thousand guests. The theatre was the first ever built into a liner and was designed to accommodate live stage presentations. The tiled indoor pool was eighty feet long, with graduated depths. The Winter Garden included sprays of water and exotic birds in cages. The Main Lounge was covered in Dupas glass panels, and special Aubusson tapestries were used to upholster the chairs. Each first-class stateroom had its own decor, resulting in four hundred individual styles, overall. Visitors aboard were invariably impressed with her elegance, quality, and spaciousness.

On August 28, 1939, the *Normandie* was temporarily laid up at Pier 88, at the foot of West 48th Street, due to the threat of war in Europe. She was never to sail again. As the Nazi war machine advanced, it seemed prudent to keep the prized liner in the security of the then neutral American waters. She sat idle—her funnels capped with canvas, her furnishings overlaid with dustcovers, and her staff reduced from 1,200 to a mere 115.

While most of the world's liners were eventually sent trooping, the task awaiting the *Normandie* remained a mystery. Rumors abounded—including one that suggested converting the ship into an aircraft carrier by gutting the interiors. On December 12, 1941, five days after the Japanese attack on Pearl Harbor, the ship was officially seized by the U.S. Government. On the twenty-seventh, after being transferred to the Navy, she was renamed USS *Lafayette* and her conversion to a troopship began at Pier 88. Later, she was to go to Boston for thorough dry-docking. The luxurious interiors were stripped and the fittings sent ashore, mostly no farther than Pier 88 itself. An incredible sense of urgency hung over the entire project.

On February 9, just days before her intended departure, sparks from a workman's acetylene torch ignited a pile of kapok life preservers. Fire spread quickly on that bitterly cold winter afternoon. Workers evacuated the ship and firefighting units both ashore and afloat arrived at the scene. Midtown Manhattan was suddenly blanketed in orange-brown smoke. Then, amidst the excitement, a fatal miscalculation occurred: far too many tons of water were poured onto the smoldering liner. In the early hours of the next day, unable to withstand the additional weight, she ripped from her moorings and capsized. In spite of her safe berth in New York harbor, the brilliant *Normandie* was lost.

On her side, the former luxury ship presented the most difficult salvage job in history. Her funnels, masts, and upper decks had to be systematically removed as large pumps pushed harbor water out of the vast, blistered hulk. This extraordinary operation, which was used as a Navy diving school exercise, was completed in the late summer of 1943, amidst more talk that the *Normandie* would now definitely become an aircraft carrier. Instead, she was towed to the 1,100-foot graving dock at Bayonne, for brief inspection, and then laid up at the Columbia Street pier in Brooklyn. Two years passed without further decision on her fate. She was stricken from the Navy's list of active ships in October 1945. There seemed to be little interest in her future, especially in view of the enormous revitalization costs. Subsequently, she was sold to Lipsett, Incorporated, a local scrap metals firm, in October 1946, and her grotesque remains were towed across New York Bay to Port Newark for final dismantling. Ultimately, this $60,000,000 ship of genius realized a pathetic $161,000 as scrap metal.

The Queen Mary

To the utter amazement of the British, in 1929-1930, the Germans swept the seas with not just one but a pair of new superliners, the 50,000-tonners *Bremen* and *Europa*.

Recovering quickly, English steamer firms planned a large-scale retaliation. First, Canadian Pacific ordered its biggest liner, the 42,000-ton *Empress of Britain*, commissioned in 1931. Soon afterward, the White Star Line signed with Belfast shipbuilders for a 60,000-tonner, intended to be called *Oceanic*. (Unfortunately, soon after construction began, the project was abandoned, a fatality of the Depression and White Star's very fragile financial state.) Her proposed running mate was to be the largest and most powerful of all, however, a 75,000-ton Cunard liner that was, it was rumored, to be named *Victoria*.

The well-known John Brown Company, at Clydebank in Scotland, had been selected as the builder and the first keel plates were laid down just after Christmas, 1930. While the early plans indicated a very large passenger ship, she would also have exceptional engines, with a projected capability of making the Atlantic run in under four days. More important, however, she was the first of a pair that would offer twin-liner express runs on the Atlantic. Previously, all passenger firms had to run three large liners to provide a weekly sailing from each direction. According to Cunard's plan, with a normal passage time of five days, their two giant partners could sail once a week from each end. Furthermore, although very little was said about it, this Cunard ship was designed to recapture the Blue Ribbon from the *Normandie*.

The havoc of the Depression (when the number of commercial passengers declined drastically, and corporate revenues plummeted) reached the Clyde by December 1931, a full year after construction had begun. Work was halted, and all but a handful of the construction crews went on the lay-off lists. The immense hull sat—silent, lonesome and guarded by a small maintenance staff. Long debates began in London over whether or not the British Government should advance monies to the financially ailing Cunard Company to continue construction of this national "wonder ship." Some ministers actually thought the entire project was wasteful, that the ship's intended passengers, the American millionaire set, had vanished. Fortunately, after over two years, the motion to extend loans was approved, and life returned to the Cunarder in April 1934.

Rumor persisted that the ship would be called *Victoria*, fol-

Outward bound, the *Queen Mary* is shown leaving New York for one of her weekly transatlantic crossings in 1963.

lowing the Cunard "ia" nomenclature (all of their earlier celebrated ships had "ia" names—*Mauretania, Aquitania, Berengaria*).
Amidst tight secrecy, however, it was decided to break tradition.
Since the nation was still caught in the bleakness of the Depression, and since the Government had underwritten a good part of
the project, it was decided that a more nationalistic, a more in-
spiring, name for the ship would be appropriate. The monarchy,
with the revered King George V and Queen Mary on the throne,
was the ideal subject. Cunard, the Government, and the Royal
Household all agreed: the new national flagship would be named
for the Queen. On September 26, 1934, their Majesties traveled
to the shipyard for the formal christening. In a ceremony using
a one-hundred quart bottle of Australian wine, the Queen named
the liner the *Queen Mary*. The secrecy had ended, and the public
applauded the choice. It would become one of the best known
names of all in shipping.

The *Queen Mary* entered service in May 1936, and soon afterward captured the Blue Ribbon from the *Normandie*. The French
liner later regained the pennant, but it finally went to the Cunarder in 1938, and she held it until the appearance of the *United
States*, in 1952. From the very beginning, the *Queen Mary* was the
most successful of all the superliners. While the others, including
the magnificent *Normandie*, never earned a financial profit, the
Queen Mary was a blazing success. No big liner has ever given
better service, developed a finer reputation, or earned more profits.

The *Queen Mary* was, of course, a ship of wonder and distinction. The 140-ton rudder had a door in its side so it might be
inspected in drydock. The anchors weighed sixteen tons and were
attached to nearly 1,000 feet of anchor chain each. There were 151
watertight compartments, 10,000,000 rivets, 2,000 portholes and
windows, and 257,000 turbine blades. The three whistles weighed
a ton each and could be heard for ten miles. There were 700 clocks,
600 telephones, and 56 different woods used on board.

The *Queen Mary*'s early commercial years were comparatively
brief, however. In September 1939, along with such liners as the
Normandie, Ile de France, and the brand-new second *Mauretania*,
she was laid up at New York, at the Cunard pier at the foot of
West 50th Street. Like the other ships, she was supposedly awaiting the end to the "political crisis" in Europe. That end was sadly
distant. The *Queen Mary* was repainted in wartime gray and then,
briefly, in March of the following spring, sat across the pier from
her brand-new counterpart, the *Queen Elizabeth*. This second

Queen—with a distinguishable two, instead of three, funnels—had just secretly dashed across the North Atlantic from her Clydeside birthplace, where she might have become an easy target for the threatening Luftwaffe. Here the two great Cunard *Queens*, destined to be the best-known superliners of all, awaited their next orders. The *Queen Mary* was, in fact, the first to depart for military service and soon sped off for Sydney, Australia, where she was to be stripped and refitted for trooping. The *Queen Elizabeth* followed her several months later, in November.

At first, both *Queens*—known during the War years as the "gray ghosts" because of their top secret movements, radio silence, and nighttime blackouts—operated across the Indian Ocean, carrying Australian soldiers for the African campaigns and then returning with prisoners, evacuees, and the wounded. In

Army nurses wave and cheer as the *Queen Elizabeth* docks in Luxury Liner Row, returning over 15,000 American soldiers and passengers to home waters in August 1945.

1942, following an agreement between President Roosevelt and Prime Minister Churchill, the pair was returned to the North Atlantic, to begin an almost weekly relay, carrying troops between New York and Gourock in Scotland. (The Channel route was far too dangerous throughout the war.) This was in preparation for the projected invasion of Europe. Compared to their intended two thousand peacetime passengers, the two liners had been restyled and adapted to carry over fifteen thousand GIs per crossing. Whole divisions, and more, could cross on the eastbound sailing of each of the *Queens*. The *Queen Mary* established the greatest record of any ship during a crossing in the summer of 1943, when she left New York with 16,683 soldiers and crew aboard. Hitler had offered an Iron Cross with Leaves and a $250,000 reward to the U-boat commander that would sink one of the giant *Queens*. Fortunately, none ever succeeded.

Soon after the victory in Europe, in the spring of 1945, the *Queens* began returning to New York with the same large loads of troops. When this postwar task was complete, they were extensively refitted and refurbished for the reopening of transatlantic luxury service. In July 1947, the *Queen Elizabeth* joined the *Queen Mary* for the first time, and Cunard's vision of a two-ship express run was finally realized. Sailing between New York, Cherbourg, and Southampton, they customarily left New York on Wednesdays and arrived in Britain by Mondays. The inbound ship would arrive at New York on Tuesdays and remain in port for about twenty-four hours before reversing this sailing process. For the next fifteen years or so, until the early sixties, the *Queen Mary* and *Queen Elizabeth* (the *Queen Mary* was always slightly more popular and more grand) were the most profitable and prestigious pair of liners afloat.

One of the more memorable aspects of service for the *Queens* was the nearly endless procession of celebrities who crossed in the ships. At New York, a press boat often greeted the incoming *Queen* in the Lower Bay. A small army of reporters and photographers would climb aboard and record the arrival, usually on deck, and with a ship's life ring clearly in sight, of a Hollywood star, political figure, or noted author. There might be Rita Hayworth or Elizabeth Taylor, the Churchills or the Eisenhowers, or Noel Coward. Newspaper centerfolds often included photos from the latest arrival of one of the Cunard *Queens*.

The ship's two thousand passengers were divided into three classes—upper-deck first class, cabin or second class, and tourist class (steerage had disappeared in the twenties). By 1960, fares for a five-day crossing amounted to some $450 in first class, $300 in cabin class, and $225 in tourist class. It was a leisurely, luxurious means of travel that was best described in Cunard's advertising slogan of the day, "Getting there is half the fun."

Beginning in the early sixties, the *Queen Mary*'s (and the *Queen Elizabeth*'s) average number of passengers, like those of most other transatlantic ships, began to decline. The age of the jetliner had arrived and had so altered transocean travel that six days became six hours. The biggest liners, especially aging giants like the *Queens*, were hard hit. Seeking alternate income, the *Queen Mary* was sent on occasional cruises to the tropics, five days to Nassau for $125. Unfortunately, having never been intended for anything

The last of the three-stackers, the *Queen Mary* had a distinguished career that spanned thirty-one years, from 1936 until her retirement in 1967. She now serves as a museum, hotel, and convention center in southern California.

but the cool, often rainy North Atlantic run, she was an "indoor" ship with very little provision for sailings in the sun. Among other problems, she lacked central air-conditioning, top-deck swimming pools, and the vast lido decks, with row upon row of deck chairs, so favored by the cruise clientele. She could hardly be a success. By 1966, the illustrious *Queen Mary* was losing as much as $2.5 million a year. Cunard soon decided to retire the *Queen Mary* and the *Queen Elizabeth*.

The *Queen Mary,* the first to go, left New York amidst an escort of harbor craft, in September 1967. No ship had ever received such a farewell. To many spectators, it was the official closing of the great transatlantic luxury trade. The *Queen Mary* had spanned several decades of change: from the heyday of the thirties, and the age of the European superliners, to the war years, to the high profits of the postwar years and the fifties, and then into the declining, jet-dominated sixties. Rumors circulated that the thirty-one-year-old liner might go for scrap, or become an Australian immigrant carrier, or, worse still, a public high school, moored along the Brooklyn waterfront. In the end, the City of Long Beach, California—far removed from any of the liner's movements, yet rich in harbor oil monies, and wanting a topnotch tourist attraction—secured the *Queen Mary,* the last of the old breed of three-stackers. Bought for some $3.5 million, which was just slightly above her scrap value at the time, she was the ideal tourist attraction.

When the deal was completed, the liner left Southampton for the last time, on October 31, 1967, with more than a thousand nostalgic passengers aboard for a final cruise. It was the longest commercial voyage of her entire career. She traveled for thirty-nine days across to the East Coast of South America, through the Straits of Magellan and north through the Pacific to her new home at Long Beach. With a thousand crossings to her credit, she would never sail again.

After exhaustive conversion work, which cost in excess of $70 million, she opened as a museum-hotel-convention center, in May 1971. Permanently moored, minus her original propelling machinery and drawing all of her power and supplies from shore, she was officially reclassified as a "building," a piece of real estate rather than a working ship. In her first year, nearly 1.5 million visitors went aboard to see the most famous superliner of all time.

The *Queen Elizabeth*, which was retired a year later in October 1968, did not fare as well. She was sent to Port Everglades, Florida, also to become a hotel and museum. This project was clouded in financial trouble. In 1970, she was sold off to C. Y. Tung, a Taiwanese shipping tycoon, who planned to convert her into a floating university and cruise ship. Renamed *Seawise University*, she was taken to Hong Kong. Just as her conversion was nearly complete, however, in January 1972, she caught fire and sank. For months, the scorched, twisted remains of the former *Queen Elizabeth* poked above the waters of a Hong Kong bay. They have long since been cut up for scrap.

The United States

The *United States* was the most technologically sophisticated liner ever built. She was totally designed just after World War II and as the result of the U.S. Government's fear of another world conflict, had to be readily convertible to a troopship should the occasion arise. As a result, she could be transformed from a 2,000-passenger luxury liner to a 15,000-capacity troopship in a matter of days. Since the Government paid three-quarters of the $77 million she cost in the early fifties, its influence was especially noticeable. While there was consideration for her role as a transatlanatic liner and peacetime symbol of Yankee brilliance, her military value was always the highest priority. Fortunately, the *United States* never had to serve as a trooper.

Despite the rather obvious fact that America was at the western end of the Atlantic run, the *United States* was the first superliner to be built by American interests. Previously, the 33,000-ton *America*, commissioned in 1940, was the largest liner to be built in an American shipyard. Earlier still, the 59,000-ton *Leviathan*, had been ranked as the largest ever to fly the Stars and Stripes, but she had, in fact, been the former German *Vaterland*, seized in World War I. The 53,329-ton *United States*, constructed at the Newport News Shipbuilding & Drydock Company in Virginia, was first floated (rather than traditionally launched) in June 1951, and was completed the following spring. She was intended to run a 30-knot, 5-day schedule, to and from Le Havre and Southampton, and then certainly to surpass the *Queen Mary*'s 31-knot record from 1938. The actual statistics from the trial runs of the *United States* were deliberately kept secret by the Pentagon. Some fifteen years later, in the late sixties, it was revealed publicly for the first time that she had managed an incredible 44 knots for at least two hours during a trial run in the western Atlantic. Technically, this would have allowed her to make European shores in under two days. Realistically, the stress of such a powerful speed on her 990-foot long hull would have caused considerable damage, possibly even cracking it. Instead, the best official record for the *United States*—and the very last attempt ever made for the Blue Ribbon—was 3 days, 10 hours from end to end, at an average of over 36 knots.

The extreme official secrecy that surrounded the *United States* for most of her life not only included exact details on her capabilities; her underwater hull was closely guarded when in drydock; only specific personnel were permitted in the engine room; and certain areas of the ship were strictly off-limits to passengers. In many ways, she was treated like a nuclear-missile cruiser.

As seen from the stern of one of the escorting tugboats, the *United States*—the fastest liner ever built— is inbound on her first arrival at New York. She is shown in the Lower Bay, just off Staten Island.

The five-city-block long *United States* was also the safest ship afloat. Almost every aspect of her design and decoration was created with safety, particularly fire prevention, in mind. Fabrics, drapes, chair stuffings, even the oil paintings, were specially treated. It was often said that the only wood objects on board were the Steinway and the butcher's block. Until the advent of the World Trade Center in the early seventies, the liner *United States* made the greatest use of aluminum in the world. In addition, to guard against partial damages should she ever be used in a war zone, the ship had two of everything—double engine rooms, electric systems, and piping.

When the liner returned to New York, on July 15, 1952, after capturing the Blue Ribbon, she was given one of the harbor's ''roaring receptions.'' A newspaper account read, ''Planes zoomed overhead and harbor vessels sent up a chorus of welcoming whistles as the ship docked at her Hudson River pier at the end of her speed conquest of the Atlantic. Fireboats spewed sunlit arches of water. Bands blared on deck and ashore. The liner's 1,651 passengers filled the decks, waving and shouting. More than 1,000 persons jammed the vicinity of the West 46th Street berth.''

Boasting the largest pair of stacks ever to put to sea, the *United States* was a familiar sight in New York harbor, being in port almost every other week, between her relays to Europe. Very often, she was featured in those double-page newspaper spreads of eight or ten liners docked together along Luxury Liner Row. Unlike the partnership of the two Cunard *Queens*, which ran a weekly schedule, the *United States* was without an adequate sister ship or running mate. Until 1964, the smaller and slower *America* acted as a supplement, but on an independent timetable.

The *United States* began to lose money in the early sixties, due to a declining trade in the face of jet competition, ever costly American maritime labor, and her own hunger for expensive fuel oils. With the prospect of yet another seamen's strike in the offing, the ship was laid up permanently in November 1969. She was sent to an unused pier at Norfolk, not far from the shipyard where she was created. Her ownership passed from the United States Lines, who decided to concentrate solely in the freight trades, to the Federal Government, who held the ship's huge mortgage.

In the decade or so that followed, various proposals were advanced to put life back into the lonely, expensive giant. These schemes included use as a floating hotel, trade fair, museum, condominium-style cruise ship, and even a roving missionary center. Even the Government had some flash thoughts: using her as a Navy hospital ship in some remote Middle Eastern base, for example.

In 1978, the liner was sold for a mere $5 million to a Seattle businessman, who planned to restore the vessel as a first-rate cruise ship (the *United States* was designed for the cold North Atlantic run, and not the sunlit tropics). Extended and often discouraging delays followed. In September 1984, with the refit contracts in hand (a process that was to be divided between West German and American shipyards), the liner first needed to be stripped of most of her original fittings. Cleverly, she was opened to a curious and nostalgic public for short tours and a large-scale auction.

Over twelve thousand visitors paid just under $8 apiece to walk through the rather desolate innards of the world's fastest liner and onetime pride of the American merchant marine, while another one thousand bid for over 20,000 different items, ranging from the bridge fittings to life jackets to the silverware. The prices varied, however—from $50 for a cabin-full of 1950s furniture to $325 for the ship's houseflag to $2,200 for a dozen crested dinner plates.

At the time of writing, the *United States* is expected to resume sailing, although for worldwide cruises, in the fall of 1987. Almost assuredly, she will again visit the Port of New York.

The France

One of Charles De Gaulle's latter-day dreams was to build just one more national superliner, a modern successor to the spirit and brilliance of the exquisite *Normandie*. To the French president, such a new ship would be a soothing tonic to a nation that, he foresaw, was soon to realize the loss of its most important African colony, Algeria. Ironically, the massive designs and costly building contracts were arranged in the mid-fifties, just a few years before the first of the jets crossed the North Atlantic and changed the face of ocean liner travel forever. Work on this Gallic supership, aptly named the *France*, might have been suspended, and the entire project abandoned, but De Gaulle wouldn't hear of it. was finished at the end of 1961, the last of the big transatlantic luxury ships designed to spend almost all of her time in traditional service. For the most part, the French preferred to ignore the more lucrative possibility of leisure cruising in warm climates. Instead, they insisted on this sumptuous link between continents.

Even as the overall Atlantic trade was foundering, the *France* immediately established an impeccable image and reputation. She was booked to capacity more often than not. The aging Cunard *Queens* and even the speedy *United States* paled by comparison. She steamed into New York harbor in February 1962 to a small craft escort, a string of official welcome dinners, and wild praises. Beneath a rather futuristic profile of two winged stacks, a single mast atop the bridge, and a sharply raked bow, the tone aboard the *France* was the embodiment of ocean-liner grandeur. She revived that nearly lost era of high living on the high seas. Her gourmet restaurant for first-class passengers was said, by Craig Claiborne, food editor of the *New York Times*, to be the best French restaurant in the world. The wines and caviar flowed freely, bellboys went about in smart red rig, and special menus were printed for the pets in the top-deck kennels (which included a Manhattan fire hydrant and Paris milestone). The public rooms were done in varying degrees of stunning modern decor. There were a circular dining room, a twin-level theatre, winged chairs, glass tables, stainless trim and contemporary French art in abundance. Her very best suites and apartments were the finest on the Atlantic—with living rooms and private dining rooms, dressing rooms, trunk rooms, triple bathrooms and even a secluded courtyard for several suites. Commuting for nearly eleven months of the year between Le Havre, Southampton, and New York, the *France* was the most popular of the final breed of superliners.

While the 66,348-tonner frequently reached (and sometimes even surpassed) her full capacity of 2,044 berths, she was much like "the ships of state" of the thirties and was never realistically expected to be a huge financial success. Her revenues were measured as much in terms of prestige and goodwill. By the early seventies, however, a new set of Parisian ministers, who governed her ever-increasing subsidies, reappraised the ship's position. While legions of loyal travelers remained, the overhead was insurmountable. Even when filled to the very last bunk, the *France* still lost money. For her final season, in 1974, she was about to realize a loss of $24 million. To the French Government, the financial assistance could be better spent on another symbol of prestige and technology, the supersonic Concorde. The *France* was withdrawn in September 1974, and sent to a backwater berth at her homeport of Le Havre.

The 66,348-ton *France* of 1962 spent almost all of her time at first on the run between New York, Southampton, and Le Havre.

Like all other out-of-work superships, the *France*'s fate was the subject of endless speculation: floating hotel, casino, Moslem pilgrim ship, Soviet cruise ship, Chinese trade fair, even a resort for Club Med. She was, in fact, sold to an Arab businessman for the most unlikely combination of gambling center and museum of French culture off the Florida coast. Actually, she never left her secluded berth at Le Havre.

The largest passenger ship in the world, SS *Norway* (ex-*France*) visits New York. She now sails in the cruise trade out of Miami.

In 1979, the Norwegian Caribbean Lines, headquartered at Oslo but operating out of Miami, shocked the entire American cruise industry by buying the ship. To most, she was unsuitable, totally uneconomic, built only for a rich government sponsor. The *France* was totally refitted, refurbished, and transformed into a large seaworthy tropic resort. Half of her costly engines were removed and her service speed halved. The number of passengers was increased and the size of the crew reduced. Far from the storms of the North Atlantic, the ship—renamed the *Norway*—now sails on weekly cruises in the sun, from Miami to the West Indies. She returned to service in May 1980, after a brief, nostalgic call at New York. She has settled down to a new life, different reputation and, after several years, financial success. Although now nearing twenty-five years of age, based on the high standard of her original French construction, her Norwegian owners are convinced that she can last until fifty.

96

The Queen Elizabeth 2

The great Cunard Steamship Company could not have been in worse trouble in the sixties. The Atlantic passenger trade, that had been the firm's livelihood since 1840, was rapidly disappearing. Simultaneously, their fleet had grown aged and less competitive, and was out of step. While in the fifties, Cunard claimed to have carried one-third of all travelers who crossed the Great Ocean, ships such as the two *Queens*, the *Mauretania*, *Caronia*, and a half dozen others, looked almost dowdy compared to the new generation of the sixties, sleek vessels like the *France*, *Leonardo da Vinci*, *Rotterdam*, and *Michelangelo*. In rather quick order, beginning in 1965, those legendary Cunarders went off either to the scrap heap or to other, often far less dignified "second lives." Meanwhile, all was not lost completely. The Cunard directors turned to their old friends, the John Brown Shipyards at Scotland's Clydebank, for a successor to the *Queen Mary* and the *Queen Elizabeth*.

Initially, Cunard thought of a traditional replacement: a mildly updated version of the original *Queens*, with three classes and near-fulltime service on the Atlantic. Then, in a flash of foresight, the plans were revised, calling for a large dual-purpose ship: six months on the Atlantic, six months in American cruising, and with distinction only between the grades of cabin accommodation. Those earlier wood partitions that separated first class from cabin class and then cabin from tourist class, would not appear. Unlike almost all previous Atlantic liners, the new Cunarder would be more of a tropical cruise ship. Certainly, her passages to Cherbourg and Southampton would be run almost entirely in the milder weather months. Onboard, there were two outdoor pools, lido decks, and an open-air golf course. Within were to be found a gambling casino, an arcade of shops, a grill room, Las Vegas floor shows, specialty lecturers, and even a health spa. It required very little effort to convert her from crossing work to cruising.

Ordered in 1964, launched in September 1967 (just two days before the *Queen Mary* left New York for the last time), and then commissioned in May 1969, the naming of this Cunarder was, for some time, a tight secret. As with the *Queen Mary* in the early thirties, rumor abounded: *Britannia*, *Winston Churchill*, *William Shakespeare* and—as at least one newspaper reported—even *Jacqueline Kennedy* were considered. Named by Her Majesty Queen Elizabeth II, whose grandmother had christened the *Queen Mary* and whose mother had done the honors for the first *Queen Eliz-abeth*, the newest Cunard superliner was called *Queen Elizbeth 2*. She is named as a successor to the previous *Queen Elizabeth*, and not for the Queen herself.

While she steamed into New York to the traditional tug and fireboat reception, there was considerable speculation, soon after the maiden voyage festivities subsided, that the new *Queen* would be nothing more than a big, expensive, white elephant. After all, the airlines had more than ninety percent of the transatlantic trade and, while the intended alternate cruising was potentially lucrative, such a large ship was indeed restricted to very few world ports. In those early years, as the ship ran her intended balanced schedule between crossings and cruises, Cunard was particularly silent on her profitability, if, in fact, there was any. It was widely reported that she was losing millions, but was secretly supported by the British Government, which had loaned Cunard a considerable amount to build her in the first place.

While other liners, such as the *Bremen, France* and *Michelangelo* eventually left service, the *QE2*—as she is perhaps best known—continued, the sole survivor on the traditional New York route across the Atlantic. Even though her five-day fares are hardly less than $1,000 per person, the ship is enjoying a substantial mid-life success. In 1983, fourteen years after her delivery, she carried more passengers to and from Europe than at any other time. In peak summers, there are sufficient numbers of nostalgic, loyal, and prosperous travelers, who prefer—and can afford—the luxury of a five-day sea voyage to a seven-hour flight. Others find that the cruise ship, fun-at-sea style of the *Queen Elizabeth 2* has strong appeal. While there can still be long hours in a deck chair with a good book (or boullion at eleven, or tea at four), there is a never-ending offering of events: from aerobics and wine-tasting to lectures on stock investing and courses on computer science. Some passengers actually complain of too little time for rest.

The *QE2* is a regular visitor to the Port of New York, sitting in towering majesty at the Passenger Ship Terminal at West 50th Street. Since 1982, her funnel device (it is not a stack in the earlier sense) has been painted in Cunard's historic orange-red and black. This link to nearly 150 years of Company history is quite important. While the original *Queen Elizabeth* sometimes used as many as eight or ten tugs, the *QE2* can often be seen with a single Moran tug alongside. The considerable strides in ship manueverability, due to such features as bow-thrusters and specialty propellers, have made this possible. Furthermore, while the first

The last of the transatlantic liners, Cunard's *Queen Elizabeth 2*, came into service in 1969 against discouraging forecasts. Fifteen years later, in 1984, her northern crossings, the last of their kind, are reported to be very profitable.

Queens drew 39 feet of water, and consequently often had as little as two or three feet between their keels and the muddy floor of the Hudson, the *QE2* draws a far more convenient 30 feet. At New York, she has no tidal restrictions.

While the *QE2* has received considerable negative publicity due to a long string of mechanical breakdowns, bomb threats, a narrowly avoided Arab submarine attack in the eastern Mediterranean, and thrashings from several ferocious Atlantic storms, her annual three-month winter world (or Pacific) cruises have attracted at least as much favorable attention. She sets off from New York each January, often on a bitter winter's night, for a ninety-day voyage to as many as forty different ports on five continents. While her capacity is specially reduced to 1,200 or so (down from the normal 1,820), some 500 passengers are usually booked for the full voyage. The other 700 sail on two- to five-week segments, meeting or leaving the ship with special air connections. While the least-expensive full-cruise fares begin at approximately $15,000, the *QE2* also offered (in 1985) the most costly shipboard accommodation of all time, $307,000 per couple in one of the two top-deck "suites de luxe."

Certainly, the *QE2*'s long cruises draw a rather special clientele. Some passengers have lived aboard the liner for months at a time. An Asian prince came aboard for a brief interport voyage with a staff of fifty. One elegant woman, who jumped over the side off Hawaii, left $2 million in jewels in the ship's safe. Another wealthy dowager spent $24,000 during the world cruise, but just in the beauty shop. Not to be forgotten are the pair of ladies who were booked in one of the $100,000-cabins, and found the room too small for all of their clothes. Overcoming their disappointment, they simply booked the adjoining room, to be used as a closet, for another $100,000.

The *Queen Elizabeth 2*—the last of the New York superliners—seems assured of a bright future.

VI ALONG THE JERSEY SHORE

W.H.M.

Bayonne Military Ocean Terminal

Early in World War II, the U.S. Navy realized that it needed a facility for the rapid loading of military stores and material, and for quick repairs to naval and merchant ships. To meet these needs, land was acquired at the eastern end of a peninsula that jutted out into the Upper Bay from Bayonne, New Jersey. Piles were driven, footings poured, and a vast area was filled and shaped to include a 1080-foot graving dock, adjacent to a series of cargo docks and warehouses. The deep water and wide-open spaces of the Upper Bay made it easy for ships to maneuver, and the generous space ashore provided room for the easy and uncluttered movement and loading of priceless war supplies.

As the pace of the Bayonne facility slackened somewhat after the war, some of the berths were often used by mothballed carriers and battleships. In 1976, the graving dock was leased to the Bethlehem Steel Shipyards of Hoboken, who wanted it to repair the new generation of tankers, containerships, and even the *Queen Elizabeth 2*. Two years later, during a major refit, the finest penthouses aboard the Cunarder were built and then placed aboard her while she lay in this dock. The graving dock is still used commercially, but by the Braswell Shipyards, Bethlehem's successor in New York harbor. Much of the military freight terminal has been closed down.

Jersey Central Terminal

Railroads—with their freight yards, passenger terminals, and ferryboats—once threaded the Jersey shoreline of the Hudson. There were large, well-known, heavily-used facilities in Jersey City, Hoboken, Weehawken and West New York, which were owned and operated by such firms as the Erie, Pennsylvania, Lackawanna, New York Central, and Jersey Central railroads.

101

The Bayonne Military Ocean Terminal, in the early fifties, when it was still a busy U.S. Navy facility, particularly for mighty battleships and aircraft carriers.

The Jersey Central Terminal, located at the foot of Johnston Avenue in Jersey City, just north of Ellis Island, saw its last trains and ferries in the mid-sixties. Unlike many of the other rail structures, however, it remains as a harbor landmark to this day. Finished in 1914, the main building—done in French Chateau style—measured roughly 800 by 400 feet and was connected to no fewer than eighteen tracks and four ferry slips, linking the trains to Lower Manhattan at Liberty Street. The adjoining facilities included a mail room, baggage room, offices, and a main waiting room. The mansard roof was crowned by a most distinctive cupola and steeple. It was threatened with demolition after the decline of Jersey Central's ferry-train operations, but somehow it survived and was carefully, and lovingly, restored in the mid-seventies, as part of the Liberty State Park project.

The ferry slips have been removed and the area converted to a waterside promenade and adjacent plaza. The waiting room has been refinished as an exhibition and performing arts space. Several annual festivals, including one for a local ethnic group and another for model railroaders, have been staged at the terminal. Unfortunately, there has been one disappointment. All of the

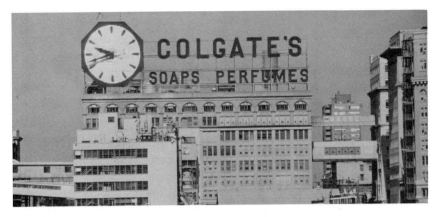

The Colgate Clock in downtown Jersey City, on the Hudson's western shore, has been ranked as the largest single-faced timepiece of its kind in the world.

original tracks were removed, thereby eliminating the possibility of the building's use as a rail museum, with authentic vintage stock.

Colgate's Clock

One of the few remaining major industries along the west banks of the Hudson is the Colgate-Palmolive Plant in Jersey City. Located just across from the towers of Lower Manhattan, the roof of the plant's largest building has contained a harbor fixture since 1924, a large octagonal clock that measures some fifty feet in width. For many years, it was the largest single-face clock in the world, covering nearly two thousand square feet. The minute hand is twenty-seven and a half feet long and travels thirty-one inches a minute. Worked by weights, similar to a cuckoo clock, the escapement is controlled by an electric clock located below, inside the plant building. An adjoining sign has recently been modernized and altered, and now features the Company's best-known product: a tube of Colgate toothpaste. Kept unlit for nearly a decade, during the energy-conscious seventies, the Colgate clock is again a nighttime attraction in the harbor.

Harborside Terminal

Sitting just across the lower Hudson from the twin towers of the World Trade Center are the twin towers of Harborside Terminal. Although far smaller in height, they are a recognizable Jersey City waterfront feature. Located just north of the Colgate-Palmolive plant, with its big clock, the terminal was built in 1929 by the Pennsylvania Railroad as a part of its enormous riverside cargo operations. Harborside Terminal was, for years, the largest cold storage facility in the world. Two 750-foot long finger piers, marked as Pier D and Pier F, jutted out into the Hudson from the main building.

After World War II, the piers and adjacent spaces were used by the American Export Lines, for their passenger and cargo ser-

Harbor tugs assist with the docking of American Export's *Exchester*, arriving at her New Jersey pier after an Atlantic crossing from Izmir, Beirnt, and Haifa.

vices to the Mediterranean and Middle East. Ships arrived from such ports as Marseilles, Cadiz, Leghorn, Izmir, Tripoli, Cochin, and Colombo. Long manifests of inbound cargo included the likes of cotton, henna leaves, walnuts, olive oil, goatskins, pepper, rubber, cinnamon, tea, cork, snails, jute, cashews, crude talc, melons, glassware, and marble chips. Later, other ships called as well: refrigerated freighters with fish from Iceland, fruit from Spain, and meat from Australia and New Zealand.

However, by the early seventies, with most of the shipping relocated to more distant Jersey locations at Newark and Elizabeth, Harborside Terminal lost much of its original work and lustre. The main building tenants declined as well, and there were reports of plans to close the entire facility. Fortunately, a decade later, by the early eighties, the forecast was reversed. Harborside was selected for major rehabilitation in the massive rebuilding program for the Jersey City waterfront. It is being converted to a modern office complex that may eventually include some four hundred marina slips along the inner bulkhead. Banking, computer, insurance, steamship, and specialty firms have leased space. Thus far, it has undergone the most extensive transformation of any of the former Hudson River shipping terminals.

Lackawanna Terminal

Prominently located in the southeast corner of Hoboken, the Lackawanna Terminal was the largest railroad terminal along the banks of the Hudson. It was also thought to be the best of its kind in the world. Now, after all the changes the port has undergone, it is the last of the working harborside "railway palaces," a monument of copper and limestone.

The terminal is actually the fifth station to be built on the same site. The current version, which opened in February 1907, successor to four earlier stations, all of which burned down, was linked to Manhattan by ferryboat and, after 1910, by the tunnels under the Hudson. It contained six ferry slips, connecting with sixteen railroad tracks. From here, Lackawanna trains fanned out, serving northern New Jersey, eastern Pennsylvania, the Pocono Mountain resorts, parts of New York State, and points west. This terminal was an instant success. It handled as many as a hundred thousand commuters a day, filling eight ferryboats an hour, during the peak hours.

It was crowned by a 225-foot tower, which originally rose from

The Hoboken terminal of the Lackawanna railroad ferries looks out over a river that saw the last of all ferry service in November 1967 when the last official crossing was made by the *Elmira*.

the center of the building. This was allowed to deteriorate, and was removed in 1948. The terminal's main waiting room, however, remains a stunning centerpiece, a space measuring 90 by 100 feet, capped by a beautiful Tiffany glass ceiling. This was painted over in 1942 when it was feared that Nazi bombers were headed for New York harbor; it was not cleaned and restored until 1981. Adjacent facilities in the complex once included a YMCA, a barbershop, a newsstand, a flower shop, a large restaurant, and even a hospital. Along the southern side, a long dock—known as the "immigrant slip"—received ferries from Ellis Island, loaded with freshly arrived Europeans. They were placed aboard Lackawanna trains for resettlement in the Midwest. A local trolley system also adjoined the terminal until 1948. Elaborate model railroad exhibits were staged in an upper level hall until the mid-fifties.

The Hoboken terminal was the home of such noted long-dis-

106

tance trains as the Chicago Limited, the Lackawanna Limited and, more recently, the Phoebe Snow. For decades, passengers and mail traveled swiftly and on schedule. When, however, in the mid-fifties, the highly lucrative mail trade began its swing to trucks, the great Lackawanna passenger train returns began their drop into the red. Dwindling passenger figures hastened the descent. In 1960, Lackawanna merged with their neighbor on the Jersey City waterfront, the Erie Railroad, and became the Erie-Lackawanna. Still more changes were in store, particularly for the Hoboken terminal. The Phoebe Snow, the best known of the latter day luxury trains, finished service forever in November 1966. A year later, the ferry run to Manhattan expired. Finally, in early 1970, the last long-distance train out of Hoboken (to Youngstown, Akron, and Chicago) ended its service. Thereafter, the remains of the Lackawanna Company were strictly for Jersey commuters. The marine division—tugs, barges, railway car-floats and floating cranes—was closed down in 1976, as were almost all the other railroad fleets. In 1979, New Jersey Transit took over the entire operation, including the terminal itself.

The new owners have had a considerate, almost loving, concern for the old building. In recent years, there has been a general clean-up, some restoration, and even the creation of a small open-air plaza on the north side. With its vintage character intact, the terminal has occasionally been used as a film set, as well. The cavernous limestone waiting room, the tracks approached through gates in distinctive wrought-iron fences, World War I commuter cars, and night scenes of floodlit, steamy platforms have contributed fantastic atmosphere to a number of films. Segments of such films as "Funny Girl," "Three Days of the Condor," "Voices," and "Gloria" have been made at the Hoboken station. Another addition is an annual railway fair (arts, crafts, antique trains, and free train rides to the Jersey Meadows and back), staged on a Saturday in October. On what would otherwise be a quiet weekend afternoon, with hardly any of the sixty thousand weekday commuters in sight, the Lackawanna Terminal comes to life—filled with balloons, music, and nostalgia.

The Hoboken Ferry

It was a misty evening, just at twilight. The Hudson seemed particularly moody, the lights of ships along the Manhattan piers began to switch on and the skyline of the financial district stood out in the dusk. The towers stood in rigid formation, much like soldiers, in what seemed to be an Emerald City. The tone was supposed to be cheerful: the Hoboken High School band blared out tunes and marches, champagne flowed, horns hooted, and all the while, camera-carrying television crews, with glaring yellow lights, filmed the occasion for posterity. It was Thanksgiving eve 1967, and the last Hoboken ferry, the *Elmira*, was on her final round trip to Barclay Street. It was also the end of ferryboat service anywhere on the Hudson—from such upriver points as Kingston and Poughkeepsie to the lower ends of Jersey City. Progress had struck again: the mass of commuters had defected to auto, bus, and subway travel. The last surviving Lackawanna Railroad ferries were giving up in the face of declining loads, high overheads, stricter safety standards, and plain old age.

Ron Buzzanca, then a trumpet player with the High School band and now a teacher in the Hoboken school system, recalled that last trip. "It was very sad. Amidst the streamers, the drinks and the cheers, I knew it was the last time that I would feel the river spray and inhale its smells. Several souvenir hunters grabbed life rings and posted signs. Then, at the very end, a solo rendition of 'Taps' finished-off the voyage. The Hoboken Ferry was suddenly gone forever."

The Hoboken Ferry was an institution. Occasionally, friends will still refer to it—sailing across from Manhattan to catch one of the Lackawanna trains, or to board one of the Holland-America liners, or simply to have a meal at the Clam Broth House. The occasional Late Late Show comically refers to it. In one of their grand musicals, even Fred Astaire and Ginger Rogers were supposed to have crossed on it.

On the Hoboken side, many long-time residents recall the ferry with fondness—and often a sense of loss. I must have crossed on it several hundred times, myself. My total infatuation with the harbor and its ships made me a frequent passenger, particularly on summer days, between the rush hours. I also made some of the early summertime evening runs, just as the sun would put firelike sparkles in the skyscraper windows.

Other memories crowd in: the distinctive curve in the shape of the ferries, the matching curve in the long benches on the passenger decks, the bright glow of the exposed light bulbs, the wooden boxes of the shoeshine men who worked each crossing, the gloved deckhands who handled the metal gates that restrained the cars and trucks until the ferry was safely docked, the

108

One of the last Lackawanna ferries, the *Scranton*, sailed between Hoboken and Barclay Street in Lower Manhattan.

captain and mate peering down from the two wheelhouses on the off-limits top deck, the churning of the backwash as the ferry approached the slip, the unforgettable music of the chains and cables as the outer pier deck was raised or lowered to match up with the main deck of the ferry as she berthed, regardless of the height of the tide. Such sights and sounds will haunt the memories of ferry buffs for the rest of their lives.

While the Hoboken ferry began as early as 1811, it was but one of many such services that later plied the Hudson. After the turn of the century, there were more than two dozen different routes. Anita Heimbruch, a former resident of Hoboken, recently recalled spending many leisurely Sunday afternoons on the Hudson. ''In the twenties and thirties, we would take the Hoboken Ferry from 14th Street and cross to 23rd Street in Manhattan. As excited youngsters, we crossed over the partition at the 23rd Street Terminal to take the downtown Hoboken boat, which sailed to Lackawanna Terminal. Then, again carefully crossing to the next boat, we sailed to Barclay Street. From there, we switched to the Weehawken ferry, which sailed to 48th Street. The four voyages cost a nickel. From Weehawken, we caught a trolley to Hoboken for another nickel.''

The Lackawanna ferries—with names like the *Chatham, Maplewood, Binghamton, Elmira* and *Lackawanna*—were the last of their kind to work the Hudson. Mostly, they're gone for scrap. Only two survive. The *Binghamton* found a new life as a restaurant in Edgewater. The *Lackawanna* sits in anchorage along the western shores of Staten Island, surrounded by derelict barges, floating cranes, and tugs. She, like them, is neglected, patiently awaiting her date with the scrappers.

Today, the Hoboken ferry lives only in history and memory.

Stevens Institute

Castle Point is the tallest natural elevation in Hoboken. It is located just south of the Maxwell House Coffee plant and the former Bethlehem shipyards, and is some six city blocks north of the Lackawanna Terminal. A small island in the days of Henry Hudson, almost the entire area now houses Stevens Institute of Technology, one of the country's foremost engineering schools. Castle Point is capped by the Institute's biggest building, the fourteen-story stainless administration tower, which replaced the Stevens family mansion, built in 1854 and mercilessly demolished in 1959.

110

The Institute grounds seem more evocative of a suburban campus than one located in the heart of a city. It is surrounded by brownstone houses and tenements, but from the grounds, one is more aware of the velvety, tree-shaded lawns, and the breathtaking view across the river to the skyline of New York City. From its commanding heights, one sees out over the urban sprawl that surrounds it. The campus contains the usual mix of dormitories, apartments, lecture halls, a large library, administration buildings, and some staff housing. Two buildings deserve special mention, however. In the especially elongated Davidson Laboratory, large-scale ship models and other nautical items are tested in huge tanks. Equally interesting is the thin green, ten-story tower that was erected down by the river at the foot of Sixth Street. This has been nicknamed the "Tower of Toilets." It is filled with toilets and other plumbing items which are tested for efficiency and water conservation from first floor controls.

In the mid-sixties, when the Institute found itself particularly hard-pressed for bed space, they bought a laid-up passenger-cargo ship, the *Exochorda*. She had been built in 1944 and had sailed under the American Export Lines flag. She had been used on the Mediterranean run and had appropriately sailed from nearby Pier B. Parts of her engines and her propeller were removed and she was refitted as a permanently-moored dormitory ship with two hundred berths for the privileged senior class. She was renamed the *Stevens* and placed just below the campus, at the former Ninth Street pier. From 1967 until 1975, she was a familiar sight along the river, especially at night when she was floodlit, and "fairy lights" were strung from her twin masts. To many, she probably seemed to be some tropic-bound cruise ship. When the student housing problem finally eased by the mid-seventies, the *Stevens* had finished her task. Sold to scrappers at Chester, Pennsylvania, she was towed off, only to return to New York four years later, in 1979, to be fully dismantled at the nearby Kearny scrapyards.

Maxwell House

Perched along the Hoboken waterfront, just north of Stevens Institute and across from Manhattan's Chelsea section (in the West Twenties), are the sand-colored buildings of the Maxwell House Coffee plant. This plant opened in 1939 and is still a thriving operation that, at peak, produces the equivalent of thirty thousand cups of coffee a minute. It is perhaps best known for its huge neon sign, which continually flashes an unchanging message to New Yorkers: ''Good to the last drop.'' Including a large illuminated coffee cup, the sign was once the largest self-lighted rooftop advertisement in the world.

The Hoboken Shipyards

One of the most noticeable landmarks along the Jersey shoreline has been the Hoboken shipyards. Positioned in the northeast corner of mile-square Hoboken, the docks were actually composed of two separate firms, the larger Bethlehem Steel Company and the adjacent Todd shipyards. Placed between the Maxwell

An expansive view of the Bethlehem Steel Shipyards in Hoboken during the early seventies.

112

House plant and just south of the former Erie Railroad yards and the Lincoln Tunnel ventilators, both in neighboring Weehawken, these shipyards stretched along six blocks of city waterfront. Tall, gooselike cranes, perched on lattice-steel platforms, hovered over as many as a dozen deep-sea ships at a time. Some of the ships remained in the waters of the Hudson while others rested in wood drydocks, high and dry, balanced on a long series of blocks underneath. Long ladders, wires, chains, ropes, and hoses were connected to these vessels. Some came for little more than a day; others, needing more serious attention, remained for weeks.

The Bethlehem Steel yard was the site of the former Fletcher, Harrison & Company, a Manhattan-based builder of boilers and engines that first opened their Hoboken facility in 1853. Forty years later, as it became the W. & A. Fletcher Company, facilities were expanded to handle larger ocean-going ships. Business prospered, sparked by the continual growth of the port itself. The name was changed again, in 1929, to the United Shipyards. It was acquired by Bethlehem Steel in 1938.

The yard reached its peak during World War II, serving over four thousand ships of all types, and with as many as eleven thousand employees. Many ships were converted from peacetime to military use and then, years later, reconverted to their commercial status. Bethlehem also maintained a floating operation, with barges and tugs (and trucks for more urgent deliveries) that serviced numerous ships while still at their normal piers. Many of these ships, such as the giant Cunard troopships *Queen Mary* and *Queen Elizabeth*, were actually far too big to use one of the Hoboken docks. They were serviced by Bethlehem work crews while at Manhattan's Pier 90. Many years later, in 1976, the Company leased the 1,080-foot long graving dock at the Bayonne Military Ocean Terminal, especially for the new generation of supertankers and containerships and even another Cunarder, the *Queen Elizabeth 2.*

During the fifties, as a very steady flow of work continued, the Bethlehem Hoboken yard ranked as one of the largest marine engine repair facilities in the country. It was the flagship of the four Company yards in New York harbor, that also included two in Brooklyn (at 29th and 56th streets) and one on Staten Island. The latter three yards were closed in a large consolidation effort in the mid-sixties.

The Hoboken yard was expanded further in the late fifties to include not only extra berths and an additional large drydock, but also a special oil-tank cleaning operation that was soon used by

113

a steady procession of visiting tankers. At its largest, the buildings and piers filled 45 acres and ran for 1,700 feet along the Hoboken waterfront. There were shops for welding and machining, for copper and piping, and for carpentry and sheet metal. There were eight tower cranes, two floating derricks, a pair of small tugs, four drydocks, six separate piers, an office, power station, firehouse, and even a small hospital.

The last boom years of the Hoboken shipyards were the sixties. There were overhauls for such famed ocean liners as the *Independence* and *Constitution*, conversions of wartime transports to contemporary containerships, and the ''jumboizing'' of some smaller tanks into bigger ones. Work continued around the clock. I can vividly recall, living as I did just a few blocks from this humming plant, the work shift whistles: 7:25 and 7:30 in the mornings, 12:00 and 12:40 for lunch and then 4:00 and 4:15 for the afternoon change. There was also an 8:00 o'clock supper whistle and a midnight call for the night crews. These whistles echoed throughout Hoboken, especially in the deep stillness of a winter's night. Early mornings were also filled with the screeching sounds of the tugs that were assisting ships in and out of drydock, or just moving them from one dock to another. The tugs were, in fact, talking to one another during the maneuvers. I can also recall the special magic of the shipyards at night: floodlit drydocks, lighted ships, illuminated funnels, and the downward columns of light from the lamps on the cranes. The welders' torches would spew out streams of fireworks-like sparks, and light up the night sky with a flickering blue light.

The Todd shipyards were finally closed in 1965 and merged with their New York operations at the Erie Basin in Brooklyn, which in turn was closed down in 1983. The Bethlehem Steel works began a slow but steady decline by the early seventies. As fewer ships called at the Port, fewer needed repairs. Then, to make matters worse, some erstwhile steady customers began to use less expensive yards in Europe and in the Far East. Simultaneously, the skilled craftsmen who had been employed by Bethlehem began to leave, spurred by the shrinking work load to other, busier shipyards and industries. As a result, the high quality of Bethlehem repairs began to slip. There had been as many as fifteen hundred workers at the yard in 1962. This dropped to seven hundred a decade later, and then to as few as three hundred by 1982.

The financially ailing Bethlehem Steel Company sold the Hoboken yard (along with almost all of their other U.S. marine operations) to the North Carolina-based Braswell Corporation in 1982. The sign at the front gate now simply read "Hoboken Shipyards Inc." U.S. Navy contracts offered work for a short time, but when the last of these expired in September 1984, the yard was closed officially. Braswell has shifted their New York operation to the single large graving dock at Bayonne. Such a limited facility is, quite sadly, adequate for current demand.

The Hoboken shipyards are soon to be demolished and replaced by a new water-front high-rise and marina complex.

Kearny Scrapyards

During World War II, four hundred ships were built at the Federal Shipyards in Kearny, located some fifteen miles west of Manhattan. Situated along the west banks of the Hackensack River, the facility has remained a familiar sight, especially to motorists who use the local highway bridges and the Pulaski Skyway.

Soon after the war ended, when their military contracts abruptly expired, the yard was faced with extinction. Instead, having been sold to the Union Mineral & Alloy Corporation, the facility's work changed from shipbuilding to shipbreaking. Some ships that had been built at Federal were scrapped at the same site, years later. In the sixties and early seventies, as the U.S. Government sold off much of its unwanted wartime tonnage, the Kearny scrapyards were among the biggest and busiest in the country.

Fourteen 50-ton gantry cranes stand along a dozen docks and have hovered over a vast assortment of unwanted craft. These have ranged from wooden hull minesweepers and coal-fired tugboats to the battleship *South Dakota* and the aircraft carriers *Enterprise* and *Franklin D. Roosevelt*. In 1973, there were so many ships waiting to be scrapped that some had to be anchored across the Hackensack, on the Jersey City shore. There were Liberty ships and Victory ships, tankers, destroyers, troopships, cruisers, attack transports, ocean-going tugs, and even several retired ocean liners, including the sister ships *Washington* and *Manhattan* of the United States Lines.

A 7,200-ton, 441-foot Liberty ship, which could be bought from Government surplus in 1970 for as little as $140,000, would be scrapped within six weeks. On the other hand, a large carrier, which would cost $2 million, might take well over a year. Once a ship was brought into one of the inner berths, the demolition would begin according to a very specific, organized plan. The stripping, from smokestacks, masts, and top decks downward, would be done by a trio of cooperating teams: the ship burners ("the torch men" as they are called), crane operators, and the ground burners. Pieces of the ship would be cut free and then lifted off, being lowered either into pier-side trucks, gondola railway cars, or barges. Some of it would then be broken up further while other pieces, such as generators, engines, and boilers, would be taken out for resale. The scrap has mostly ended up in the steel mills of the Midwest; the resale items have sometimes gone to other ships. The yard owners have also quietly negotiated sales with nostalgic, former servicemen and crew members who wanted remembrances from "their" ship. Bridge instruments, brass fittings, and cabin furniture have been particularly popular.

When a ship has been cut quite close to the water line, the final remains are gradually hauled ashore and then cut up, down to the last nut and bolt. Only a crane operator and handful of workers have witnessed the last rites, as the final sections of hundreds of ships have been pulled from the water, never to sail again.

By the late seventies, work had declined considerably for the Kearny scrapyards. The Government has had fewer ships to sell off, and the risk from asbestos has become a major concern. At the same time, some other out of work ships have gone to more aggressive overseas scrappers, especially the Taiwanese, the world's mightiest ship scrappers. Spain, Italy, and even Pakistan are in the bidding as well. Consequently, the Kearny yards, which were handling eight ships at once, and using five hundred workers in 1973, were down to a single ship a decade later. Rumor has it that since the Government plans to sell further "mothball' ships to foreign scrappers, the Kearny operation might close completely.

Other Changes Along the Jersey Shore

Until the sixties, the sixteen-mile stretch from Jersey City, just south of the Statue of Liberty, to Edgewater, a mile or so below the George Washington Bridge, bustled with maritime life. There were crowded riverside railroad yards, smoking factories, hundreds of nestled barges, coal docks, ferryboats, shipyards, a scrap metal works, and even a terminal especially designed for

116

off-loading bananas. But, as the harbor's emphasis shifted to the more efficient containerized systems, the once necessary auxiliary harbor craft (and businesses) of floating derricks and lighterage barges, railway carfloats, and a huge fleet of tugs lost their work. Many firms simply collapsed and left their craft to rot, sink, or sometimes burn to charred ruins. The railroads abandoned their freight yards, which also became the victims of neglect and, often, fire. Many factories were emptied by owners and tenants, who deserted for more sophisticated plants in the suburbs. By the end of the seventies, there was very little that remained of the busy, pulsing boom years of the Jersey waterfront. A new, totally different shore line is ahead, however. It is being planned for the needs of the twenty-first century.

The former Greenville Railway yards in Jersey City, located just southwest of the Statue of Liberty, is to become a 300-acre industrial park. An adjacent coal port was under consideration, but was eventually dropped, due to potential environmental problems.

A Swiss-based organization plans to build sixteen hundred houses, a hotel, and offices along specially made curving canals at Caven Point, also in Jersey City. Originally, the area was used as a major ammunition depot for military ships. More recently it has served as the home base of the Army Corps of Engineers.

The Morris Canal, which is just north of the Central Railroad Terminal, and below the Colgate-Palmolive plant, was for decades the home of derelict barges, houseboats, and a small shipyard that could handle nothing larger than a Staten Island ferry. Completely cleared in recent years, it is destined to become Liberty Harbor North, a housing complex with as many as twenty-five hundred units. Exchange Place, a small former business and factory area that adjoins Colgates and the Harborside Terminal, is to become the site of several new office buildings, with a combined total of 1.8 million square feet.

The old Erie and Pennsylvania Railroad yards began their deterioration in the sixties. Except for the opening of a small tugboat repair facility, the area has seen little revitalization. Beginning in 1985, it is to become the combined Harsimus Cove and Newport City developments, with high-rises and townhouses containing over eleven thousand units, marinas, and a major shopping complex. When completed, it will reach north through downtown Jersey City to the Hoboken City line, at New Jersey Transit's Lackawanna Terminal. By itself, Newport City will cost $2 billion.

The long empty Hoboken steamship piers are to be rebuilt as

117

part of a $500 million scheme of apartment towers, offices, a ho-
tel, and still more marinas. Work starts in the fall of 1986.

The Weehawken waterfront is also scheduled for transformation. The old Weehawken freight yard of the Erie Railroad was
taken over by the Seatrain Lines container ship operation, which
went into bankruptcy in 1981. On this site, Hartz Mountain Industries is backing a new development called Lincoln Harbour.
This will include 1.5 million square feet of office space, 250 housing units, a 300-room hotel, a marina, and several waterfront restaurants. A bit farther north, just past the Lincoln Tunnel
ventilator shafts, and taking in part of the long-abandoned New
York Central Railroad yards, trucking tycoon Arthur Imperatore
has plans for his $3 billion Romulus Development. Preliminary
sketches suggest several seventy-story towers, a monorail, cable
cars, and a revived commuter ferry service to Manhattan's West
Thirties.

Roc Harbor, consisting of still more luxury housing, both high-
rise and townhouse style, a marina, and another projected ferry
run to Manhattan, is planned to replace the Lever Brothers plant
in lower Edgewater. Two other remnants from the bygone days
of an industrial Hudson waterfront, the 800-foot long Ford Motor
Company plant and pier (from which, until the fifties, thousands
of American-made cars were shipped overseas), and the 14-floor
Alcoa Aluminum Building, which began its decline in the late sixties, are both to be replaced by still more housing. The Ford pier
is to become Edgewater Commons; the Alcoa site will, it is hoped,
become the home of a high-priced condominium tower.

Many of these projects are still to be finalized and will, no
doubt, be altered somewhat before construction starts. Their
overall completion will take at least twenty years. The total cost
is estimated to be in the neighborhood of $10 billion. As demo-
lition begins, and the new complexes start to sprout, little will be
left to indicate that the Jersey Shore of the Hudson was, so recently, a bustling, busy, working waterfront.

Computers, Containers, & Car Carriers

In the twenties, when the Port Authority of New York & New
Jersey bought the marshlands along Newark Bay, they could not
have envisioned its eventual use and distinction as the largest
container port in the United States. The container era did not begin for another thirty years, until the mid-fifties. Even then, it

took another decade before it began to expand noticeably. In the early sixties, Manhattan's Department of Marine & Aviation wanted to redesign and rebuild the city's finger piers for this new age in cargo shipping. Unfortunately, this scheme had two very important drawbacks: woefully inadequate adjacent space for marshaling containers and, to make matters worse, the city's poor financial situation. Port Newark and Elizabethport, as the two areas in New Jersey were named, were far better suited. The Port Authority was quick to develop a large plan for adaptation of these areas and the construction of new facilities. So satisfactory were they that after the first container ships went to these Jersey berths, some fifteen miles west of New York City, almost all others soon followed. The growth since the fifties is, perhaps, best exemplified by the almost incredible increase in container-ship design and

One of Sea-Land's first ships, the converted breakbulk freighter *Fairland*, had a total capacity of 226 containers.

construction. In 1955, Sea-Land's 468-foot long *Fairland* could carry a maximum of 226 containers, which required some fifteen acres of adjacent shore-side space for parking and maneuvering. By 1970, the Farrell Lines' 813-foot *Austral Entente*, with a capacity of 1,700 containers, required fifty acres. By 1978, five container terminals at New York handled two million of these "boxes," which the containers are often called. Over 80 percent of all cargo which now comes in and out of New York harbor is in container ships, two-thirds of which use either Newark or Elizabeth.

Containerization was developed as a vastly improved system of shipping. One large contemporary container ship can do the work of six or eight earlier break-bulk freighters, and with far more efficient (and less expensive) port handling. Some container ships are in port for fewer than twenty-four hours compared to the five or six days required by many cargo ships in the fifties. The Elizabeth container port, which is often called the "container capital of the world," has been a great success. The facilities cover nearly twelve hundred acres. There are two dozen large container cranes and twelve giant cargo distribution buildings, with over a million square feet of floor space. There are also more than fifty other miscellaneous structures. Other smaller container shipping facilities have been built around the port: the Global Marine Terminal in Jersey City; Howland Hook on Staten Island; and one each at Red Hook and 39th Street in Brooklyn. One other terminal, Port Seatrain in Weehawken, was closed after a decade of operation, and is being rebuilt for office, housing, and recreational spaces.

Port Newark, which started as the first major container port, has become a diverse shipping area with facilities for bulk cargo, fruits, scrap metals, and, most notably, the arrival of large quantities of imported cars. Often they come in shipments of as many as 6,000 aboard boxlike car carriers, ships which are as long as 800 feet and displace over 35,000 tons.

The centerpiece of New York Harbor's deep-sea shipping is now at Elizabeth and nearby facilities. The initial transition, which began in the sixties, spelled the slow decline, and then complete demise, of the once busy finger and shed piers of Manhattan as well as those of Jersey City, Hoboken, Staten Island and, to a large extent, Brooklyn. Noted facilities, such as Manhattan's Chelsea docks, Jersey City's Harborside Terminal, the Hoboken Port Authority piers, Staten Island's Clifton and Stapleton docks, and Brooklyn's Bush Terminal and Erie Basin, were doomed to obsolescence by the coming of the container ship. In addition, the once vast lighterage, floating crane, railroad marine, and tugboat systems have all but disappeared as well.

The perpetual, vibrant bustle of the New York waterfront in the days when a major ship was said to be in- or outbound every twenty-four minutes, is no longer evident. Cargo shipping at areas like Elizabeth, while still diverse, impressive, statistically important, and highly profitable, now moves at a smoother, quieter, more effortless pace.

VII   SOME FAMOUS CARRIERS

W.H.M.

Cunard Line

In November 1838, the British Admiralty invited tenders for steamers that could deliver mail across the North Atlantic at regular intervals. A copy of the advertisement fell into the hands of, among others, a prosperous Nova Scotia merchant named Samuel Cunard. He was intrigued by what he read and quickly made his way to London. With an extraordinary business sense, he promptly secured the contract, which was valued at £50,000 per year, for a twice-monthly schedule of sailings from Liverpool to Halifax and Boston, and back to Liverpool. In preparation, Mr. Cunard ordered a quartet of brand new paddle steamers. Thus began one of the most famous shipping companies of all time, the Cunard Line.

The first of these ships, the 1,100-ton *Britannia*, crossed the Atlantic on her maiden trip in July 1840. Made mostly of wood, this little vessel could fit quite comfortably on the foredeck of the present *QE2*. She had two decks, accommodation for 115 passengers, and spaces for 225 tons of freight. With a service speed of 8½ knots, she ran the passage between Liverpool and Boston in 14 days, 8 hours. She was soon followed by three sister ships and then, with Mr. Cunard's optimistic predictions of continued success, by several other vessels.

In the 1850s, Cunard was already established as a major transatlantic firm. The Company was quick to adopt two revolutionary developments in steamer design: the use of iron and then steel, replacing wood for hull construction, and the use of the screw propeller, which ousted the earlier paddle wheel. The *Andes*, of 1852, was the first Cunarder to be constructed of iron and the first to have a single screw propeller. While the Company extended its service to the Port of New York (to Jersey City, in fact) in 1847, demand and the competitive spirit of the Atlantic trade prompted successively larger and faster ships. The 3,300-ton *Persia*, completed in 1856 and touted as the world's largest ship, was three times the size of the *Britannia*, which had been commissioned just sixteen years before. The 7,400-ton *Servia*, of 1881, was the first Cunarder built of steel. The wooden paddlers, the sail ships, and even the iron ships soon disappeared forever. The *Servia* was also the first Cunard ship to be fitted with electric light. An ever present sense of luxury was also an important ingredient. Along her two upper decks, she had 202 staterooms for 480 first-class passengers (steerage passengers used lower deck quarters). The larger cabins had wardrobes, dressing tables, and double beds, and marked the beginning of shipboard "suites de luxe." The 7,700-ton *Umbria* and *Etruria* were the Company's first team of express liners, ships capable of over 20-knot service speeds. A decade later, by 1893, still larger and faster express ships were added, the sisters *Campania* and *Lucania*, with top runs of over 23 knots. Cunard's reputation grew steadily. In 1890, during their fiftieth anniversary celebrations, a major newspaper noted, "Cunard is the epitome of ocean steam navigation, and it is not very long since nearly every liner that crossed the Atlantic carried on her bridge, or in her engine room, at least one man who had served in a Cunard ship."

The *Campania* and *Lucania* were not only the fastest ships of their day, but quite remarkable for their size, luxury, and regularity of service between Liverpool and New York. In 1901, Marconi carried out his first experiments with wireless transmission aboard the *Lucania*, and, two years later, the same ship had the first shipboard newspaper with contents received by wireless. Between 1895 and 1905, Cunard added no fewer than fifteen ships, representing a total of nearly 139,000 tons. The decade ahead was to witness the widespread use of the wireless, the successful application of the more efficient steam turbine, and finally, the creation of two of the most famous liners of all time, the 32,000-ton sisters, *Lusitania* and *Mauretania*, of 1907.

The new super express ships were built with financial help from the British Government and operated with a subsidy. They regained the Blue Ribbon and other prized distinctions, all of which had begun to fall into German hands in 1897, when the North German Lloyd introduced their *Kaiser Wilhelm der Grosse*, a 14,300-tonner, a record breaker and the first of the four-stackers. A succession of German superliners had followed that were bigger and faster still. Cunard's intention was to run a trio of giant liners that would provide a weekly sailing in each direction. The 45,000-ton *Aquitania* joined the earlier team in 1914.

Immigrant children arriving in New York aboard Hamburg American's *Imperator* in 1913, before the ship's name and career were changed as a result of World War I.

During World War I when Cunard liners served as troop transports, hospital ships, armed merchant cruisers, depot ships, and one even as a seaplane tender, the Company transported over a million troops and over ten million tons of cargo. Unfortunately, over 20 ships, totalling some 200,000 tons, were lost in action.

The twenties saw several changes: the conversion from coal to oil fuel, thereby permitting far more efficient operation, the elimination of steerage, and the creation of tourist, or improved third class, and the addition of no fewer than thirteen new passenger ships. Most notable of these was the 52,000-ton German *Imperator*, which came to the Company as reparations, and began a highly successful second life as the *Berengaria*. Cunard had been providing regularly scheduled service from London and Liverpool to New York, Boston, Halifax, Quebec, and Montreal. With the addition of the *Berengaria* to the *Mauretania* and *Aquitania*, they could now provide a weekly trip each way between Southampton and New York. These three ships were the last word in 1920s travel, and were frequented by celebrities from all walks of life.

In the late twenties Cunard began planning for the pair of superliners that would be fast enough to provide a twin-liner express run—the brilliant *Queen Mary* and the *Queen Elizabeth*. World War II saw them serving as the outstanding troopships of all time.

Winston Churchill declared that the two *Queens* "helped to speed the end of hostilities in Europe by at least a year."

By the mid-fifties, Cunard had renovated and rebuilt its fleet, and was said to carry a third of all passengers who crossed the North Atlantic. The *Queen Mary* and *Queen Elizabeth* ran nearly year-round between New York, Cherbourg, and Southampton; the *Mauretania* had slightly longer sailings that called at Cobh, Le Havre, and Southampton; the *Caronia*, which made periodic crossings, ran mostly on long, luxurious cruises (in fact, she was the first major liner to be designed for full-time cruising); the *Britannic* traded between New York, Cobh, and Liverpool; the *Media* and *Parthia* ran a direct service to Liverpool; and a brand new foursome, the *Saxonia, Ivernia, Carinthia* and *Sylvania*, sailed from Montreal and Quebec City to either Greenock and Liverpool or Cobh, Le Havre, and London. At New York during the summertime peak season there were often four passenger sailings a week.

Cunard, now a member of the London-based Trafalgar Group, is presently much more a leisure firm than a transportation company. Even the *QE2*, which continues about half the year with the highly popular Atlantic crossings, is run mostly as a cruise liner, making leisurely trips to Bermuda, the Caribbean, the Mediterranean, and North Cape, and an annual three-month trip around the world. The *Cunard Countess*, a 17,000-tonner added in 1976, spends her entire year in the West Indies, operating out of San Juan, while her sister ship, the *Cunard Princess*, runs summer sailings to Alaska from Vancouver and winter cruises from Los Angeles to the Mexican Riviera. Cunard added Norwegian America Cruises, in 1983, and now includes the luxury cruise ships *Sagafjord* and *Vistafjord* in its schedules.

Nearly one hundred and fifty years since its inception, Cunard—a name steeped in maritime history—continues its long-established service to New York.

Moore McCormack Lines

New York shippers Albert V. Moore and Emmet J. McCormack started service with a $5,000 investment, a single office, and one small freighter, the *Montara*. The year was 1913, and the ship steamed off on a rather worrisome voyage with a cargo manifest that included a shipment of dynamite. Her destination was Rio de Janeiro. It was the beginning of the seventy-year history of the Moore & McCormack Company, which later became the

Moore McCormack's luxury cruiseship *Brasil* made regular sailings from New York to South America as well as the Caribbean, the Mediterranean, and Scandinavia.

Moore McCormack Lines, one of the best-known steamship firms under the American flag.

The Company expanded rapidly, abetted by financial backing from J. P. Morgan and others. By 1917, it had fifteen annual sailings to South America. Services were expanded to such ports as Bahia, Pernambuco, Recife, Salvador, Santos, Montevideo, and finally as far south as Buenos Aires. Mor-Mac, as it was commonly abbreviated, also added a transatlantic freighter division, the American Scantic Line, which traded to Oslo, Gothenburg, Copenhagen, and Helsinki. This line later helped turn the little Polish fishing village, Gdynia, into a major Baltic port. Some of the American Scantic ships, such as the *Scanmail, Scanpenn, Scanstates* and *Scanyork,* also carried ninety passengers apiece on the Scandinavian run. In winter, they cruised to the West Indies.

Moore McCormack itself entered passenger ship service in 1938, with another subsidiary, the American Republics Line, which had three 20,000-ton liners—the *Argentina, Brazil* and *Uruguay*—on the 33-day "Good Neighbor" run from New York to Trinidad, Rio de Janeiro, Santos, Montevideo, and Buenos Aires. These ran until 1958.

During World War II, the Company offices managed over 150 ships for the U.S. Government, which were sent on over 2,000 voyages, carrying one million troops and twenty million tons of cargo. Afterward, sailings were resumed with new breeds of war-built freighters, ships of the C3, C2, and Victory classes. There were usually three sailings a week from New York: one to the major South American ports as far south as Buenos Aires, another only to Brazilian cities, and the third on the northern run for American Scantic.

In 1957, Mor-Mac added the Robin Line, which ran a freighter service to South and East Africa, to ports such as Capetown and Durban, Beira and Mombasa. This meant an additional weekly sailing from the Company's Brooklyn piers. A year later, in 1958, the Company added the 22,000-ton sister ships *Argentina* and *Brasil* to replace the 20,000-tonners of 1938. High-standard ships, with deluxe, first-class accommodations for all 553 passengers, they plied the South American run and also did considerable cruising: around Africa, in the Mediterranean, in the Caribbean, and on summer trips to Scandinavia and the Northern cities.

During the sixties, the Company added fast new freighters, replacing most of the postwar tonnage. Its aim was to compete effectively with foreign flag lines, especially the new nationalized Latin American fleets, and forerunners of the container age. Considerable changes were still to come. The American Scantic service began to lose money and was discontinued. The Robin Line operations were absorbed totally into Moore McCormack and, thereafter, used only Mor-Mac ships. Finally, in 1969, the passenger cruise division was closed out, a decision prompted largely by ever-increasing costs for American-flag ocean liners. Barely a decade old, the *Argentina* and *Brasil* were laid up at Baltimore, and several years later, were sold to Holland America Cruises, who refitted them as the *Veendam* and *Volendam*. Freighter service, often with twelve passenger berths, to South America and South Africa was all that remained for Mor-Mac thereafter.

As merchant shipping has become increasingly competitive and specialized, Mor-Mac's independent position had to be seriously evaluated if the firm was to remain cost-effective. In 1983, as part of a large pooling agreement to create a more profitable worldwide service network, the company and its ships were sold to the United States Lines. Unfortunately, in the process, the original name—and even the names of the ships themselves—were changed to suit the new parent company. The once famous name of Moore McCormack is no longer in use at the Port of New York.

Holland-America Line

The Holland-America Line was founded in February 1871, and started operations across the Atlantic to New York in October 1872. Their first ship was the 1,700-ton *Rotterdam*, an iron-clad screw-type vessel with capacity for just over 300 passengers. Prosperity quickly followed. Within a decade, the company's ships had landed an impressive 10,000 passengers per year at New York, which represented an average of 550 per voyage.

Holland's premier transatlantic firm from the very beginning, they developed a sound, sturdy, and conservative reputation within the shipping community. Unlike the neighboring Germans or the dominant British across the Channel, the Dutch were not very keen on overly large, fast, or luxurious ships. For their biggest building program to date, in 1900–02, they added three fine but moderately sized sister ships, the 12,000-ton *Potsdam*, *Rijndam* and *Noordam*. Their accommodations reflected the passenger trade of the time: 300 or so in first class, some 200 in second class, and, most profitable of all, 1,800 berths in steerage. While the company expanded and became still more profitable, they remained somewhat cautious on the future of the ocean liner.

When the 17,000-ton steamer *Nieuw Amsterdam* came into service in 1906, she was the last liner still fitted with a set of sails.

Holland-America's scheduled service from Rotterdam and Channel ports to the port of New York (Hoboken, to be exact) continued without interruption until the depth of the Depression. In the early thirties, while their overall image was still very strong and popular (they were known as the "Spotless Fleet"), their Atlantic passenger loads—like those of almost all other firms—dropped drastically. Rather than withdraw several liners, the Company turned to one-class cruises to Bermuda, the Caribbean, and the Mediterranean, carrying mostly those Americans who were able to weather the economic storms. Highly successful, Holland-America promptly developed its second very strong reputation. It was now both a transatlantic and a cruise organization. In its continuous efforts to improve services, the company employed some of the very first cruise directors, those shipboard officers who organize activities and diversions for the passengers during leisure sailings.

The company produced its best liner, one of the world's most beloved, in 1938, the 36,000-ton *Nieuw Amsterdam*. A stunning showcase of national art and design, she joined the other "ships of state" of the thirties as the representative of the Dutch. Her career, which continued until 1974, was one of the most successful of all ocean liners.

After World War II, part of the company's revival was the addition of two noteworthy passenger ships, the sisters *Ryndam* and *Maasdam*, of 1951–52. They were the first Atlantic liners wherein tourist class was given as much as 90 percent of the accommodations; first class was limited to a very small, upper-deck section. The huge success of these ships set a standard that was soon copied by many Atlantic lines.

By the late fifties, the Holland-America fleet consisted of the "Big Three"—the aforementioned *Nieuw Amsterdam*, the *Statendam* of 1957 and the luxurious *Rotterdam* of 1959—which ran a weekly service from New York to Southampton, Le Havre, and Rotterdam; the *Ryndam* and *Maasdam*, which also included Cobh or Galway in Ireland, as well as extensions to Bremerhaven; the passenger-cargo ships *Noordam* and *Westerdam*, which ran a direct nine-day service to Rotterdam; a subsidiary fleet of low-fare student and immigrant ships; and also a sizable fleet of freighters, which delivered, among other goods, large quantities of cheese, tulips, and beer to the Port of New York. It was not until 1971 that the North-Atlantic passenger crossings were eliminated and the freighter services consolidated into newly-formed consortiums of containerized shipping lines.

The Holland-America Line became Holland-America Cruises and continued with full-time cruise services out of New York, but mostly on southerly courses—to Bermuda, Nassau, and the West Indies. The 38,645-ton *Rotterdam*, which, like the other ships, was re-registered to Curacao in the Dutch West Indies, also ran an annual three-month trip around the world. While the company moved its headquarters first from Rotterdam to Stamford, Connecticut, and then, in 1983, to Seattle, the *Rotterdam* upholds the Dutch link with Manhattan, one that has lasted over 110 years. In January 1986, as she set sail on her 25th annual world cruise, she gained the added distinction of having made the greatest number of such luxury sailings, for a major liner, from New York.

United Fruit Company

They were known, in the past, as the "Great White Fleet," words which were spelled out in a large rooftop sign on one of the first finger piers along Manhattan's Lower West Side. The United Fruit banana boats were smartly kept and almost always white, prompting many harbor admirers to think of them as more like tropic yachts than commercial ships.

The company's roots trace back to 1870, when Captain Lorenzo Baker, master of the schooner *Telegraph*, delivered 160 bunches of bananas on a two-week north-bound run from Jamaica to New Jersey. The popularity of such tropical fruit was soon established, and Baker, together with several early partners, formed the Standard Navigation Company. By 1885, a specialized importing firm, the Boston Fruit Company, was added. Additional ships joined the fleet, plantations were bought in Jamaica, and the demand, especially for bananas, accelerated. By 1898, the company's ships delivered over 16 million stems in U.S. ports.

While the Boston Fruit and Standard Navigation companies dominated the banana market in the northeast, its chief rival for the lower East Coast and in the Gulf, was the N. C. Keith Company. Keith used New Orleans as a major port of entry for bananas from Central America. Later, in 1899, the latter firm's financial problems prompted a merger between the two rivals, and resulted in the creation of the United Fruit Company, or "Fruitco." Expansion was rapid, and included extended port facilities, not only at Boston, New York, and New Orleans, but also at Baltimore and Philadelphia, and later along the West Coast. It also acquired a considerable number of plantations in the Dominican Republic, Honduras, Guatemala, Cuba, Panama, and Columbia. In 1902, it began acquiring shares in the Elders & Fyffes Company, Britain's largest banana shipping firm. Ultimately, this firm, too, became wholly absorbed into United Fruit.

While the company's earliest ships used fresh air piped through ventilators to the lower deck banana cargos, the first of the new, greatly-improved, refrigerated banana boats—the *Esparta*, *Limon*, and *San Jose*—arrived in 1904. Each could carry 45,000 stems of consistently cooled bananas. Each also had space for 18 first-class passengers, the beginning of United Fruit's interest in liner service, both for port to port schedules and for roundtrip cruises.

Years later, in the twenties and thirties mostly, the company added larger, more efficient, ships as well as separate subsidiaries, including the Honduras-registered Mayan Steamship Company. After World War II, some eighteen brand-new ships, of the 7,000-ton *Fra Berlanga* class and the 5,000-ton *Yaque* class, were built. These ships and their sisters were familiar visitors to New York harbor, arriving at the specially-built banana exchange terminal at Weehawken, and then shifted to one of the lower Manhattan berths to load general cargo for the return run.

By the late sixties, however, these ships were transferred to foreign flag subsidiaries and eventually scrapped. They were the last of United Fruit's American generation of banana boats. The company, which was renamed United Brands, gradually reduced its New York service and finally relocated to Albany, a port considered superior, geographically, for the distribution of bananas. While some banana boats still pass through local harbor waters, often displaying the original United Fruit funnel colors, they are mostly chartered craft, with home ports like Hamburg, Monrovia, and Yokohama.

United States Lines

The present-day United States Lines, with its current headquarters in suburban Cranford, New Jersey, can trace its roots to 1871. In that year, the American Line was formed, with the financial help of the mighty Pennsylvania Railroad. The company, engaged in the busy North Atlantic passenger, freight, and mail services, soon prospered and grew. They owned several of the finest liners on the transatlantic run, including the *New York, Penn-sylvania, St. Louis* and *St. Paul.* This was to become, certainly, the most important company to carry the Stars and Stripes on the Atlantic in direct competition with such giant firms as Cunard, White Star, Hamburg-America, and North German-Lloyd.

Soon after the turn of the century, the American Line joined with another national shipper, the Atlantic Transport Company, and together they formed the basis of the International Mercantile Marine, one of the largest shipping combines of all time. Head-quartered at One Broadway, in the heart of New York's early shipping industry, and just across from the brand-new Customs House at Bowling Green, this combine was led by financial wiz-ard J. P. Morgan. Its scope soon extended to several prominent British firms, including the White Star Line (who would build the legendary *Titanic*), the Leyland Line, the Dominion Line, the Oceanic Steam Navigation Company, and the Shaw Savill & Al-bion Company. At its peak, the IMM—as it was often called—had 120 ships of some 1.3 million tons under its control.

After World War I, the United States Lines (as it had, by now become) included such ships as the 59,900-ton *Leviathan* (the for-mer German *Vaterland*), which had been taken as a prize of war and remains, to date, the largest liner to fly the red, white, and blue. She sailed on the express route to Cherbourg and Southampton, competing with the big trios for Cunard and White Star. There were also the sister ships *President Harding* and *Pres-ident Roosevelt*, which traveled to Hamburg, and the seven sisters of the little *American Merchant* class, which were routed either to London or to Liverpool and Glasgow.

Hard hit by the Depression, the financially ailing *Leviathan* ran reduced service for a time, then was laid up, and was finally sold for scrap in 1938. Her replacements were more moderately sized passenger ships, the sisters *Manhattan* and *Washington* of 1932–33, and the *America* of 1940.

During the fifties, the United States Lines and its subsidiaries, the American Pioneer Line, the Panama Pacific Line, and the South Atlantic Line, ran over fifty cargo ships and two famed transatlantic liners, the aforementioned *America* and the brilliant *United States*, of 1952, the last holder of the Blue Ribbon. Each carried three classes of passengers: first class, cabin class, and tourist class. The liners sailed from New York to Cobh, South-ampton, Le Havre, and Bremerhaven. The freighters included those same ports as well as Glasgow, Liverpool, Dublin, Ant-werp, and Hamburg. The American Pioneer ships ran out, via

The containership *America New York* needs four Moran tugs to turn it at Howland Hook, Staten Island, when leaving the port.

132

Panama, to Yokohama, Kobe, Pusan, Manila, and Hong Kong, and later, southward to Auckland, Wellington, Melbourne, and Sydney.

The postwar freighter fleet was largely replaced and consolidated in the mid-sixties. As the container age took hold, the company left its Manhattan terminal, at the Chelsea docks in the West Twenties, and relocated to the brand-new 200-acre facility at Howland Hook on Staten Island. The passenger service ended in 1969, when the *United States* was laid up at Norfolk, and transferred to U.S. Government ownership. All of the remaining conventional cargo ships soon gave way to an all-containerized fleet. In 1979, the United States Lines closed their lower Manhattan headquarters, severing their only remaining link with the past.

At present, the United States Lines—a division of McLean Industries—runs one of the most sophisticated container services in the world. The fleet is headed by a brand-new series of 950-foot long container ships, the *American New York* class, which first appeared in mid-1984. With a capacity of 2,241 containers each, they are the largest ships of their type ever built.

Seatrain Lines

In January 1929, a revolutionary ship, the *Seatrain*, was commissioned. She was the result of a brand-new concept in ocean

Docking in an obscure berth along the Hudson at Edgewater, New Jersey, the long flat-looking ships of the Seatrain Lines were served by a crane capable of lifting fully loaded railway "box cars."

133

transport devised by business partners Graham H. Bush and Joseph Hodgson. They felt that to save time and dockside labor costs, fully-loaded railroad freight cars could be loaded directly aboard deep-sea ships. On that first sailing, the *Seatrain* departed with the equivalent of a mile-long freight train on board.

The initial run had been between New Orleans and Havana. Services soon expanded to include New York, Savannah, and Texas City. A pair of specially-built, larger sister ships were added in 1932, and another set in 1940. Special heavy-duty lifting cranes were built and first placed in the port of New York at Hoboken and then at Edgewater. Ships fully loaded with the brown-colored "box cars" of almost all the American railroads, and bearing such names as *Seatrain New York, Seatrain New Jersey, Seatrain Georgia, Seatrain Louisiana* and *Seatrain Texas*, left New York as often as twice weekly until the late sixties. During World War II, these specialized craft were especially useful in hauling tanks, trucks, and other large vehicles. The *Seatrain Texas,* having rushed through U-boat infested seas with 250 heavy tanks and other urgently needed cargo, is credited with helping to stop the Nazi advances in North Africa.

When Seatrain was merged with other New York-based shipping interests in the mid-sixties, the overall fleet expanded to three dozen ships, including the 115,000-ton supertanker *Manhattan,* the first commercial deep-draft vessel ever to navigate the Northwest Passage (1969). Seatrain entered container shipping in the late sixties, and soon terminated its original railroad shipping service. The Edgewater facility was abandoned and a new complex created in Weehawken, on the site of the unused Erie Railroad freight yards. Service routes were extended throughout the world, and, at its peak, some sixty thousand containers were in use. The company also had interests in ship chartering and management, port operations in the Middle East, a shipbuilding plant located in a portion of the original Brooklyn Navy Yard, as well as holdings in oil, coal, and petrochemicals.

Regrettably, the Seatrain shipping services collapsed in 1981. A declining North Atlantic trade, increased competition, and greatly inflated operating costs were contributing factors to the demise. The ships were decommissioned, the containers auctioned off, and the decade-old Weehawken Terminal closed. That site is scheduled to be rebuilt as housing, recreational, and commercial space.

Hapag-Lloyd

A group of German shippers formed a packet company in 1847, to run a direct service between Hamburg and New York. Officially, it was named the Hamburg Americanische Packetfahrt Actien Gesellschaft or "Hapag," but was best known as the Hamburg American Line. The company's first vessel was the fully-rigged sailing ship *Deutschland*, which could carry twenty cabin class passengers and two hundred in steerage. The immediate response was such that other ships were soon added.

A decade later, in 1857, another German shipping company was formed, the North German Lloyd. Based at and sailing from Bremen, they were the chief rival for Hapag's sailings from Hamburg. The Lloyd's first passenger ship, the 2,600-ton *Bremen*, arrived at New York on her maiden call on July 4, 1858, with twenty-two cabin passengers, ninety-three in steerage, and 150 tons of freight. On her return crossing to Bremerhaven, which took twelve days and five hours, she was noted as having made the fastest passage on record. It was the beginning of both companies' interest in speed, passenger luxury, distinction, and increased tonnage. Hapag's *Elbe*, for example, had cut the passage time to eight days and twelve hours by 1881. Increasingly larger and faster liners followed.

After his visit to the British fleet, and specifically to the record-breaking White Star liner *Teutonic*, at Spithead in 1889, Kaiser Wilhelm II returned with a very specific goal: German liners must be made to surpass their British counterparts. North German Lloyd responded first, by 1897, with the first of the four-stackers, the 14,300-ton *Kaiser Wilhelm der Grosse*. She was the world's largest ocean liner to date, and captured the coveted Blue Ribbon as well. With a crossing to New York of just under six days, she snatched the pennant from Cunard's *Lucania*. Other "German monsters," as they were called, soon followed. They grew larger, faster, and more luxurious. The *Deutschland* was commissioned by Hapag in 1900, the *Kronprinz Wilhelm* in 1901, and the *Kaiser Wilhelm II*, in 1903, for North German Lloyd. The final member of these four-funnel record breakers, the Lloyd's *Kronprinzessin Cecilie*, appeared in 1906, just a year before all honors went back to the British, with Cunard's new 31,900-ton *Lusitania* and *Mauretania*.

Hamburg America and North German Lloyd shared one of

New York's largest terminals, located along a four-block stretch of waterfront in Hoboken. It seemed virtually self-contained, with workshops, storerooms, an engine plant, a coal shed, a smithy, a painter's shop, a large baggage department, fifteen offices, a separate railway, and a rooftop apartment for the Company superintendent.

In 1913, Hamburg America prepared to introduce the first of an awesome trio of superliners, in fact the largest ships ever created. The *Imperator* arrived first, in June of that year, and had a tonnage in excess of 52,000 and a capacity for more than 4,500 passengers. Larger still, the 56,000-ton *Vaterland* followed in June 1914, but was barely in service when World War I erupted. The

Hapag-Lloyd's *Europa*, the former Swedish *Kungsholm* of 1953 purchased by the German firm in 1965, was the Company's last cruiseship to sail regularly from New York. She was rerouted to European sailings only after 1971.

third ship, the *Bismarck*, bigger still at 56,500 tons, never saw German service and sat out the war years at her shipyard berth. When the hostilities ended, all of her intended Hamburg America and Lloyd fleetmates were either sunk or seized as reparations. The *Imperator* went to the British and became Cunard's *Berengaria*; the *Vaterland* fell into American hands and became the *Leviathan* for the United States Lines; and finally, the *Bismarck* was completed, but for the British, to become White Star's *Majestic*. The only surviving liner still in German hands by 1920 was the mechanically unsound *Deutschland*, launched in 1900.

Recovery and rebuilding took some years, but triumph and glory were again returned to the Germans by 1929. North German Lloyd, making a remarkable recovery after the devastation of the war, introduced the first of a pair of huge superliners, the 50,000-ton *Bremen*. The 49,000-ton *Europa* followed in 1930. They retook the Blue Ribbon from the British, held by Cunard's *Mauretania* for no less than twenty-two years. It was the beginning of the grand heyday of "the ships of the state," the greatest age of the superliners.

World War II was equally devastating to the two largest German shippers. The *Bremen* burned at her Bremerhaven pier in 1941, and the *Europa* was seized by the Americans during the Allied invasion in 1945; it was subsequently given to the French, becoming the *Liberte*. All that remained of the earlier fleets were a few coastal freighters, tugs, and barges. Several years later, freighter service was resumed on the New York run, but with rather small ships. The first postwar passenger ship, the *Berlin*, the former Swedish *Gripsholm* from 1925, reopened liner service in 1955. Another *Bremen* was added four years later.

With the traditional transatlantic passenger trade winding down in the face of increasing jet air service to and from Europe, Hamburg America and North German Lloyd merged and became, officially, Hapag-Lloyd. Instantly, their combined fleet was one of the largest in the world. While they continue to run cruise ships, their original service between Hamburg and Bremerhaven and the United States is carried on by a fleet of fast, high-capacity container ships. The first quartet of 24,000-tonners, which maintained weekly sailings from each direction, were a vast improvement over earlier models. In performance, they were the equal of two dozen conventional freighters of the fifties.

With nearly one hundred and fifty years of service across the Atlantic, Hapag-Lloyd continues to serve New York.

Grace Line

The first of the Grace-owned ships to sail from New York to the West Coast of South America were large sailing ships known as "Down Easters." In good weather, the run to Valparaiso in Chile via Cape Horn took 100 days. It was not until 1892 that the Company turned to steamers and ordered a quartet of ships that would make the same passage in 38 days. After 1914, with the opening of the Panama Canal, sailings required less than four weeks.

While the Grace Line developed considerable cargo ship interests, hauling coffee, bananas, and fish, they are perhaps best remembered for their *Santa* passenger liners. The most popular of these were a foursome, the *Santa Elena, Santa Lucia, Santa Paula* and *Santa Rosa.* These were built in 1932–33, in the very confines of New York harbor, at the Federal Shipbuilding yards at Kearny, New Jersey. They were notable for their high standard of accommodation. All of their first-class staterooms had private bathrooms and beds instead of bunks. The dining room, situated amidship on the Promenade Deck, was more than two decks high, with tall casement windows and a dome that rolled back, giving the effect of a breeze-swept outdoor café. Waitresses rather than waiters did the serving.

By the end of World War II, there were nearly two dozen *Santas* in service, and more were added subsequently. These were mostly cargo ships with sumptuous cruising accommodation for fifty-two passengers. Their routes varied in length from twelve to forty days, depending on whether they were just in the Carribean, or whether they went through the Panama Canal and down the west coast of South America to Valparaiso, Chile. There were at least three Grace Line sailings from New York every Friday. In the early sixties, Grace also pioneered in the use of containers on the Pacific side of South America.

Grace's shipping division (W.R. Grace & Company are still in petrochemicals) was bought out by the Prudential Lines in 1971 and was known, for the next four years, as the Prudential-Grace Lines. In 1978, the remains of the Grace fleet were sold again, this time to the Delta Line of New Orleans. At the time of writing, because of further mergers, transfers, and withdrawals, there is little that remains of the original Grace Line fleet and its ships. Those once familiar *Santa* names are no longer heard in New York harbor.

138

Three or four Grace Line ships departed from New York every Friday until the late sixties. In this view from the mid-fifties, the liner *Santa Paula* is outward bound on a two-week Caribbean cruise while just beyond, the freighter *Santa Rita* is headed for a more extended trip, to ports along the west coast of South America.

Furness-Bermuda Line

In 1919, Britain's large Furness, Withy & Company bought the little Quebec Steamship Company, which had been operating a rather limited service between New York and Bermuda with a converted military cruiser, the *Charybdis*. Furness renamed their new acquisition the Furness-Bermuda Line. It was to become one of New York's most popular passenger companies. Under the new title, service began in November 1919.

At first, two small former Australian coastal passenger ships, renamed the *Fort St. George* and *Fort Victoria*, seemed adequate. Prompted, however, by American Prohibition, which greatly increased the lure of foreign-flag ships, and by the short sea route (a mere six hundred miles, or about forty hours steaming time) to Hamilton, Bermuda, the new service gained enormous popularity and considerable success by the mid-twenties. Some passengers preferred to sail south, remain ashore for a time, and then return on a later voyage; others made the round-trip passage as part of a one-week holiday.

In ocean liner annals, the *Queen of Bermuda* has the distinction of having sailed as a one-, two-, and three-funnel ship. Her highly popular six-day cruises to Bermuda were, with the obvious exception of the war years, run from 1933 until 1966.

Larger, more luxurious ships were soon required. The 19,000-ton *Bermuda* was commissioned in 1927, and was to be followed by the *Monarch of Bermuda* in 1931. Unfortunately, the earlier ship was destroyed completely by fire when only three years old, and therefore, had to be replaced. The *Queen of Bermuda* was ordered and first appeared in 1933. With first-class standards equal to those of many of the big North Atlantic liners, these ships—known as "millionaires' yachts"—made twice-weekly sailings from Manhattan and at peak popularity carried as many as 4,500 passengers a month to Bermuda. Round-trip fares began at $50 in the mid-thirties.

After World War II, the *Queen of Bermuda* was joined in 1951 by a new teammate, the 13,500-ton *Ocean Monarch*. Their Saturday afternoon sailings were very well known, and the two ships often proceeded together to the open Atlantic. The *Queen* went to Hamilton; the *Ocean Monarch* to St. Georges. Occasionally, during the summer months, there were special cruises to the Canadian Maritimes and the St. Lawrence River. Likewise, in deep winter, occasional cruises were made to Nassau and the Caribbean islands. Every cabin on both Furness liners had private bathroom facilities, a considerable novelty in the early years of the cruise industry.

In the mid-sixties, Furness-Bermuda was hard hit by changing conditions. New, more modern cruise ships had arrived, jets offered competition for the Bermuda vacation trade, and the U.S. Coast Guard was preparing revised, more severe, safety regulations for older passenger ships. The company would have to build two brand-new passenger liners in order to stay in business. Instead, with great regret, Furness-Bermuda chose to end its long-standing popular service. The *Ocean Monarch* was sold off to the Bulgarians for further cruise sailings, while the veteran *Queen of Bermuda* made her last run in November 1966, before going for scrap. Furness-Bermuda briefly ran an all-freight service, but soon withdrew completely.

American Export Lines

The Export Steamship Corporation also began operations in 1919, but with several small Hog Island class freighters. Their interest was in the Mediterranean, and in due course they would become the dominant American-flag carrier on that run.

Until 1931, the company's activities were limited, almost completely, to cargo transport, but in that year they added four brand-new sister ships, the *Excalibur, Excambion, Exeter* and *Exochorda*, which had very fine first-class accommodations for 125 passengers in addition to their freight capacity. Nicknamed the "Four Aces," they worked a regular 46-day round-trip service from New York to Marseilles, Naples, Alexandria, Tel Aviv, Haifa, Beirut, Haifa, Alexandria, Piraeus, Naples, Leghorn, Genoa, Marseilles, Boston, and home to New York. Many passengers used the full voyage as a cruise.

In 1936, the company changed its name to the American Export Lines and a year later added American Export Airlines, the first aviation company to offer non-stop transatlantic service. This subsidiary was sold off soon after World War II.

Sadly, three of the original Aces were lost in wartime action and, soon afterward, the surviving *Exochorda* became the *Tarsus*, the flagship of Turkey. A new quartet of Aces were built in 1944, and following military duty, were comissioned for commercial service in late 1948. They carried the same popular names: *Excalibur, Excambion, Exeter* and *Exochorda*. With similar, high-standard accommodations for 125 guests, and space for some 6,000 tons of cargo, they were augmented by no fewer than twenty-four freighters, many of which had space for a dozen passengers. There was the specially built *Exporter* class, the slightly smaller *Extavia* class and several Victory class ships. Their sailings went into the Mediterranean, to such ports as Barcelona, Algiers, Tripoli, Alexandria, Izmir, Lattakia, Piraeus, Mersin, Rijeka and Marseilles, and also beyond the Suez, to Karachi, Bombay, Cochin, Calcutta and Colombo.

The Company's passenger division expanded in 1949 with the addition of the 609-passenger *La Guardia*, a converted wartime troopship. Soon afterward, she was replaced by two new 29,500-tonners, the 1,000-passenger sister ships *Independence* and *Constitution*. They ran a three-week express service linking New York, Algeciras, Naples, Genoa, and Cannes. Another liner, the *Atlantic*, a converted freighter, was added in 1960 for extended service to Piraeus and Haifa.

The Isbrandtsen Company, another U.S.-flag shipper, acquired a controlling interest in American Export in 1960, and two years later, a new title was adopted, the American Export-Isbrandtsen Lines. Isbrandtsen was involved until 1973, when American Export returned to independent status. The liner division was phased out in 1969, due to declining trade requirements caused by the jet, and to the vastly increased costs of

The Statue of Liberty, photographed in April 1986. She now lifts a new torch, covered by several pounds of gold leaf, and will be illuminated by exterior lighting only. (Photo: Allan Litty, Flying Camera)

operating American-flag liners. New container ships were added, not only for the Mediterranean run, but for service to Northern European ports as well.

American Export was bought out completely, in 1978, by the Farrell Lines, a New York-based firm with years of experience in the African trade routes. The combined fleet was increased to forty-six deep-sea ships. The merger had one further effect: the American Export name has since been dropped completely.

Sea-Land Service

The Sea-Land Corporation, then known as the Pan-Atlantic Steamship Company, commissioned the world's first container ship, the 10,000-ton, converted, wartime tanker *Ideal X*, in the spring of 1956. On April 26, at the Marsh Street pier at Port Newark, the first cargo of its kind, 58 truck trailers, were loaded aboard the ship. It was the beginning of a revolution, a total change in the shipping industry, that would spread worldwide.

This was a bold venture, one that succeeded from the start. It was a no-frills, "shoestring," "shoebox" operation. The company's offices were in a converted quonset hut at Port Newark. Yet, as early as 1956, it only took them two days to load, just about halving the time a ship needed to sit idle in port, and greatly reducing the time and manpower needed to get the unloaded cargo away from the pier and to its ultimate destination. According to one company executive at the time, "I think you could say that back then it was like something you read about in a science fiction book, never quite imagining that it could become a reality. The history of containerization has been a marvelous march of events, a wonder in the field of transportation."

So confident of its future and importance, Pan Atlantic soon ordered the conversion of four traditional breakbulk freighters, the *Gateway City*, *Azalea City*, *Beauregard* and *Raphael Semmes*, into "trailerships." The order was promply increased to eight ships, and these became the world's first "cellularized container ships," the first to carry containers both above and below deck. Their capacities were placed at 226 "boxes," as containers are called. On-board container cranes were added, as well, enabling these ships to call at almost any port where a trailer truck could be driven alongside. At the time, very few ports had shoreside container cranes.

By 1962, the company, by then renamed Sea-Land Service,

144

The Sea-Land Company owns a total of 83,000 containers, many of which pass in and out of the Port of New York.

had moved to larger, more efficient facilities at neighboring Elizabethport. It added the "queen of the container ships," the *Elizabethport*, another converted tanker with the impressive capacity of 476 containers. Fleet expansion thereafter was continuous. Two former Grace Line ships were added in 1965, and redesigned, with space for 225 containers. The 609 foot-long, C4J Class were added in 1965–66, and were followed by the even larger C4X Class, of 1968–69, with capacities as high as 622 containers.

In the summer of 1969, five brand-new container ships, by far the biggest then contemplated, were ordered from Dutch and West German shipyards. Known as the SL7 Class, they had capacities of 1,096 containers each, twenty times more than the original *Ideal X*. Three additional 944 foot-long sisters were added as well and, by 1972–73, Sea-Land was the largest and busiest container shipper in the world.

Sea-Land's current fleet includes some of the most efficient cargo vessels afloat, including their D9 Class, which can make a round-trip voyage from California to the Far East and return without refuelling. At top speeds of 22 knots, they are propelled by efficient, cost effective, "state of the art" Diesels. With the many changes in container-ship design and construction over the last twenty-nine years, they are now larger, faster, and more efficient than ever. According to Sea-Land, however, "The fundamental purpose and the way they carry cargo has not changed. Containerization, like the light bulb and other technological breakthroughs, has been greatly improved, but remains fundamentally the same." Sea-Land remains a world leader, with a 60-ship fleet that can carry a total of 27,000 containers, at any one time.

VIII FISHERIES OF THE PORT

F.J.D.

IT IS AN AGE-OLD ritual, waiting for the tide to change in an open boat in order to pull up the fishing nets, a type of labor that has changed little since biblical times. I sit, camera hung from my neck, out of the way in Ronnie Ingold's boat, protected from the early morning drizzle by a green foul-weather suit that still carries the identification letters in large block type, US NAVY, left over from World War II. What makes this common act so uncommon is the background. Instead of the open ocean, or the rock-bound coast of Maine, it is the skyline of the west side of Manhattan, and the fishermen are out after the famous Hudson River shad.

There's a feeling of security in seeing the annual spring run of the shad, members of the herring family, coming in from the Atlantic Ocean to the Hudson River to spawn—a sense of permanency found only in nature. The first white settlers found the Indians on the river bank waiting for the buds of the trees to bloom, thereby announcing the return of the shad to their birthplace, and this spring Ronnie Ingold of Edgewater, New Jersey, is still carrying on his annual ritual.

At one time the west shores of the Hudson River, from Weehawken to Alpine, New Jersey, just north of the George Washington Bridge, were lined with hickory poles sticking out of the water, but now there are only two stake rows left to catch the silver fish swimming upriver, both tended by Ingold's fishermen. Ingold's father once had four fishing camps on the river and employed twenty-seven fishermen and three cooks, but that's all past history now.

Ron is the last fisherman from Edgewater to go out after shad. As he sits and drinks coffee aboard an old railroad barge that serves as a base on the mud flats off the shore at River Road, Ronnie talks about the river he loves, problems with pollution and PCB,* the large investment it takes today to set out his nets, and heavy losses from river traffic hitting the stake rows.

*Polychlorinated Biphenol, a suspected cancer causing chemical agent.

The shad poles are upstream in the Hudson River from the George Washington Bridge.

The annual migration of the shad is one of the mysteries of nature on the Hudson, like the salmon run on other rivers. The fish travel the Atlantic from Florida to the Gulf of Maine, moving with the changes in water temperature, preferring approximately 40° F. Although they mix and swim with others of their species from the Connecticut and Delaware rivers, and Chesapeake Bay, they'll always return to the river of their birth, when they reach four to five years of age, to continue the life cycle.

Each female has up to five hundred thousand eggs to bring upriver, when she mates with one male. Nature provides the abundance of roe to offset the heavy losses from suffocation on the river bottom and from predators, especially eels. The young that hatch stay in the river for the summer, while the spent adult fish, now worthless as a catch, return downriver, back into the Atlantic, and then head north. When the river temperature starts to drop in September, the by now three to four-inch shad have reached a point where they can cope with the open seas and follow their parents downriver to the ocean.

The fishermen turn out of their wooden bunks on the barge, after a short sleep following the last lift of nets during the night on the river. Rusty Stewart—Ingold's partner for the last few years—and the others don sweaters, yellow slickers, and boots as protection against the cold, rainy April weather on the Hudson. Most of the fishermen are youngsters who come to work for Ingold for the four to six-week season, depending on how long the fish run. At one time the shad run would draw profesional, itinerant fishermen down from the Great Lakes, but now it's just those who are between school and other jobs.

The fishermen go out on the river in open wooden boats, made especially for shad fishery. They're twenty feet long, with a high, sharp bow, an outboard motor in a well in the center, and a long square stern to give plenty of room to lift the nets. Since they fish during the night, the boats have battery-powered lights hung from overhead pipes. Out by the first pole at the end of the tow, near the Palisades shore, the fishermen wait for the tide to ebb. Although there are tide tables, the exact time is affected by the winds and local conditions on the river.

It's a strange feeling fishing in the Hudson, with the buildings of Manhattan on one side, and the cliffs that the Indians called the "Great Chip," on the New Jersey side. The constant hum of traffic drifts down from the George Washington Bridge, but for the most part, there is little water traffic or noise, and the overcast river is very peaceful. The boats are rafted together, and while the crew dozes, Ingold keeps putting an oar into the water

The square-sterned boats are made especially for shad fishing.

to test if the river flow has slowed before he starts the first lift of nets. The normal crew on each boat is three men, two working the net off the pole on the stern, while one man maneuvers the boat with the motor forward. The fish hit the net in schools, getting trapped in the diamond-shaped weave, pushed against it by the incoming tide. The trick is to gauge the tidal flow just right, lifting the net as it starts to slow down, before the fish can free themselves.

As the fishermen purse the five-inch weave net off the first pole the fish fill the floor of the boat for a good haul. The bucks bring little return to the fishermen, so as many as possible are dumped back into the river. The fish in the boat are exhausted from fighting to get off the net and battling the river current and they lie passive. Although Ingold is reluctant to discuss his gross from each lift made, an educated guess comes to about $2,000.

The fishermen take about an hour to lift the nets and load the fish from the two stake rows. Each row is like a fence across the river, with thirty hickory poles, spread out twenty feet apart, covering some twelve hundred feet across, with a gill net that hangs on heavy rings twenty feet deep. The male shad average sixteen to nineteen inches, two to four pounds, while the valuable females are eighteen to twenty-five inches and four to eight pounds each. Ron Ingold likes to boast that the fish he catches are only hours out of the Atlantic Ocean when they hit the stalls at the Fulton Fish Market, near the East River on South Street, in Manhattan.

The hickory poles used to string the nets are stored in the mud near the barge all winter, picked up in the spring, and driven fourteen feet into the river bed. Each pole costs three hundred dollars, while the nets run about twenty-five hundred dollars each. Ingold tries to protect the rows with old traffic cones during the day and lights on the poles at night, but they're still run down by passing boats operating out of the channel and straying into the area put aside by the U.S. Army Corps of Engineers for the fishery.

At one time Ingold could sell much of his catch at a roadside stand, but that was before the PCB scare. The General Electric Company plants at Hudson Falls and Fort Edwards, N.Y., on the upper Hudson, were major users of PCB and they legally dumped the chemical waste in the river for years. The chemical was banned in 1972, after it was suspected of being a carcinogen for animals. The PCB's have the nasty property of not ever breaking down; traces have been found in Arctic ice, mother's milk, and of course

The shad fishing fleet at the Fulton Fish Market, taken at the turn of the century.

151

the river bottom and fish. Ron says the shad he catches are safe because they are short-time visitors to the river, and even while spawning upriver, live off their own stored fat, eating little from local waters.

Each year there is always the question of whether the Department of Environmental Conservation will come out with new standards and close down the fishery in Edgewater. If you ask where the shad comes from in fish stores and restaurants in Manhattan the answer will nearly always be "down south," or the Delaware River, for no one wants to admit they're fished out of the Hudson River in view of Manhattan.

The Fulton Fish Market

When Ron Ingold lands his catch, it's placed in boxes, iced, and then loaded on a truck for the trip into Manhattan and the Fulton Fish Market. All the fish coming into the market today arrive by truck, mostly large eighteen-wheelers. Then smaller trucks take the purchased fish from the market to retailers and restaurants. In the not too distant past, when high liners (fishing boats with a good catch) up and down the northeast coast had

The Fulton Fish Market when the catch was landed from sailing smacks on the river side and hauled in by pulleys.

Fishermen take time out for gossip while anchored at the Fulton Fish Market.

filled their holds with a full catch, they would run up the "Gully," a canyon etched deep in the floor of the Atlantic Ocean by the currents of the Hudson River, to reach New York Harbor. The boats would then sail up the East River, to a point below the Brooklyn Bridge, and dock at the Fulton Fish Market in Manhattan.

In the early part of the nineteenth century, when the market was still young, the river and waterfront was filled with sailing vessels, schooners and smacks that brought the fish to South Street. Then, the need for speed to reach the market and get the highest price for the fish, changed the fishing fleet to trawlers, first with steam engines, and then Diesel power plants.

Today the Fulton Fish Market is over one hundred and fifty years old, still the largest wholesale market for fish in the world, and still doing business on Manhattan's lower east side, which it now shares with the trendy new stores and restaurants of the South Street Seaport. The variety of fish handled at the market is much greater now than at any time in history. Many of the more exotic species are flown in from all parts of the world to New York airports. Although much of the fish is caught outside of New York Harbor in the Atlantic Ocean, boats dock in New Jersey and Long Island and ship the catch by truck.

153

The river side of the market is now being rebuilt as part of the development of the museum area, with a retail market and restaurant hanging out over the river on the piers that once held the fishing boats.

The F. V. Felicia

The last boat to deliver a regular catch to the Fulton Fish Market was the *F. V. Felicia*. She had New Bedford, Mass. painted on her stern, but she seldom saw that port unless repairs were needed on her winch. Not only was she the last boat to dock at the market, but she was truly a New York boat, having been built at Mullers Boat Works, a family run yard that is still doing business on Mill Basin, Brooklyn. A typical wooden hull vessel, the *Felicia*, powered by a Diesel engine, was 114 gross tons, 91 feet long, with a 20-foot beam. When first built, she had the traditional two-masted schooner rig of a trawler, but her owners had her converted in 1953 to a single-masted scallop boat.

Going aboard the *Felicia* during one of her short stays in port at the Fulton Fish Market dock was like going back in time. I would often meet Jim Tobin, who had shipped out from his native Newfoundland, had fished for fifty years, and now retired, liked to visit the boat. He had sailed aboard her many times over a thirty-year period and knew all about the little boat. Jim called her "a wooden ship with iron men." He sailed as her chief engineer and had outlived two Diesel power plants installed on her. The work was hard, six hours on watch and six off while at sea, tending the Caterpillar Diesel, and like everyone else on the boat, including the cook, working the gear for the nets on deck and then pitching in on the never-ending job of shucking scallops.

The *Felicia* still used a canvas riding sail to steady her when working the nets, and the ratlines, running up the orange mast to the crosstrees, looked strange against the background of Manhattan office buildings. The living quarters used by the crew was really a forecastle in the true sense of the word, with wooden two-high bunks tucked into the bow and the center part of the small afthouse. Hot water was aboard, but no showers for the eleven to fourteen man crew, many of whom had been recruited from the party and charter boat fleet at Sheepshead Bay, Brooklyn.

Most fishing for scallops was done off the Jersey shoals, for the boat was a bit old to go to the Georges Banks any more. After the catch was brought aboard and the scallops were shucked by

154

the crew, the shells were thrown overboard to the fishing grounds, for young scallops attach themselves to the shells. The *Felicia* would sail with a cargo of twenty-five tons of ice in the summer to preserve the catch, which was packed in forty-pound bags for landing at the market.

The old scalloper would dock at Pier 18, now just a memory, at the side of the "Tin Building," built by the Fulton Fishmongers Association in the late 1800s. The New Fulton Fish Market, the building now in use, replaced a structure that fell into the East River. The last I heard, the *Felicia* was still sailing out of the New Jersey shore area, but she'll never come to New York again, for there's no room for fishing boats at the Fulton Fish Market any more.

The fishing boat *Felicia* unloads her catch at the Fulton Fish Market before the pier was removed. Now fish are delivered only by truck.

The Westway Project

The fishing vessel *Tiffany* made a good living in the winter of 1983–84 in the Hudson River. The boat never sold a fish, returning all the catch to the river, for she was part of the striped bass fishery study mandated by the courts before construction could start on the Westway Project, on Manhattan's west side, a roadway along the Hudson River.

Plans for Westway have been around since the early 1970s, but seem to be constantly held up for a variety of reasons. In 1973, the northbound lane of the old Miller elevated highway was so far gone that it collapsed, dumping a large truck into the street below, in the vicinity of 14th Street. An inspection of the roadway proved it so dangerous that it was closed down from the Brooklyn-Battery Tunnel north to 42nd Street. Interstate 478, the official name of Westway, can only run between these two points to qualify for the 90 percent Federal funding.

If the construction unions and contractors were delayed in making money on Westway, the planners, engineers, public relations people, government agencies, and even printers, have done well with all the studies that have been made. The striped bass study cost the taxpayers $3.1 million. A 1974 study had covered the environmental impact of the project, but the water quality part glossed over the fishery issue. As a result of the fishery study later mandated by the court, the U.S. Army Corps of Engineers concluded that the two hundred acres of landfill and roadway could be built, even though the striped bass might be adversely affected, but environmentalists may still hold up the project.*

The study covered the river from the lower bay to Peekskill, New York. The work provided employment for two other vessels besides *Tiffany,* the *Atlantic Twin,* and *Eastern Welder,* at a cost of $600,000 for the three boats and fishermen. The sampling required trawls in near the piers, including some under them, and then out in midstream as a control. On one trawl the boat pulled up a TV set. There was a constant problem of ripping nets caused by debris on the Hudson's bottom.

When the scientists and fishermen landed the fish they would count the different species and then dump them back into the river after tagging some. It was a strange mix of high-tech, math, science, and computers, with simple otter trawling.

*The project was killed in 1984.

156

It is understandable that early studies of the water quality discounted any large concentrations of fish in the Hudson, for the river has been receiving the outfall from twenty-three sewer pipes since as early as 1850. Treatment plants are being built, but like Westway, they too are far behind schedule. It appears that the salinity and water temperature—which stays about 30° to 32° F., even in winter—and the oxygen content of the Hudson River create an ideal wintering environment for young bass for the first two years of their lives. A great deal is to be learned from the migration patterns of the striped bass. Commercial fishermen fear that what happens in the Hudson will affect the livelihood of boats working the south shore of Long Island and Long Island Sound. It will be a long time, however, before there will again be draggers working the Hudson River waters off the shores of Manhattan.

The Sheepshead Bay Fleet

The Borough of Brooklyn, in New York City, conjures up many different images to outsiders: the City of Churches, the famous tree that grew there, the Dodgers, and of course the Great Bridge. Few people realize, however, that Brooklyn is home for one of the largest fishing fleets on the East Coast, in the community of Sheepshead Bay. The "Bay" as it is known locally is situated on the southern shore of the Borough, protected on its south from the waters of Rockaway Inlet by the peninsula of Manhattan and Brighton beaches. This location gives the area an ideal anchorage, with natural protection against the weather yet easy access to the Atlantic Ocean and nearby fishing grounds.

The Dutch first discovered the advantages of the area as a home for a fishing fleet, and it started in the ensuing years to grow steadily as a small port and farming community. Then, in 1910, the area was transformed overnight, when a large racetrack was built, and it became a playground for the rich during the Gay Nineties. The main street, still called Emmons Avenue, after a local farmer, became known as Millionaire Row. When race tracks and betting were outlawed by the State of New York, the fishermen, along with seafood restaurants, returned to the Avenue. The real impetus for growth came, however, from the convenience to the subway for Sheepshead Bay. At the same time, other points on the Brooklyn shore had lost their fishing fleets.

Around 1925, Jake Martin, a steamship master, discovered a

Above: The Sheepshead Bay party boat fleet in port after a day's fishing. The *Chief* is a converted ex-Navy boat. *Below:* One of the "Pin Hookers" prepares his catch for sale to customers who will meet the fleet.

group of sunken coal barges off the Atlantic City coast that provided a great breeding ground for sea bass. He outfitted the *Glory* as a party boat and put one hundred fishermen on the 95-footer for a trip to the bass grounds. This was the start of the party and charter boat fleet that continues to fill the piers on Emmons Avenue to this day. While the nation suffered from the great Depression fishermen filled the boats out of Emmons Avenue, night and day, going for bass in the summer and cod in the winter. A man could spend $2.50 for a day's enjoyment and bring home fresh fish for the family's supper, too. There was the added attraction of the fishing pool, still in use today, where each passenger put in a dollar, and the lucky angler who landed the biggest fish could win up to two hundred dollars in prize money, a great sum in the 1920s and 1930s.

In 1934, assisted by the W.P.A., the city rebuilt the waterfront. In 1940, Brooklyn's Belt Parkway was completed to the north of the Bay, and made for easy access by car. The fleet today varies from boats like the *Sea Wolf*, a forty-five-footer carrying thirty people at $12 a head, to the *Tampa VI*, with air conditioning, restaurant and lounge, and even color TV, built at a cost of just under $1 million, with a fare of $18 per person. The boats are run as open party boats, taking aboard anyone who has the fare, and charter boats, restricted to members of clubs, organizations, etc., who reserve the entire vessel. Business on both types is built on repeaters, regular fishermen who keep returning to the same vessels.

The high point of the day on Emmons Avenue occurs at about 4:00 P.M., when the boats return. People flock to the docks to buy fresh fish when they hear the horns of returning vessels as they enter the Bay. Crew members, called "Pin Hookers" by commercial fishermen and customers, sell off some of their catch to anxious buyers on the dock, who get a bargain compared to prices in retail stores.

Captains and crews of the party and charter boats sailing out of Sheepshead Bay feel very much a part of the American fishing industry. These men are fishermen and seafarers in the highest tradition, even though they only sail out of Brooklyn carrying day-trip fishermen.

Sailor Ed Moran, for many years a volunteer at the South Street Seaport Museum. He is now a resident at Sailors Snug Harbor, a retired seamen's home.

IX SHIPS and BOATS THAT SAIL NO MORE   F.J.D.

THE LATE CAPTAIN Alan Villiers, author, master in sail and steam, historian, and veteran of the Royal Navy in World War II, said that it was a difficult business sailing ships and boats across the oceans of the world. The only business he knew that was tougher was saving them when their sailing days were over. The Port of New York and New Jersey, like most major seaports, has its share of successes and failures in preserving historic vessels when they can no longer make their way in serving the purpose for which they were built. There seems to be no end of people who discover an old derelict, fall in love with its past, and try to make it pay for a future. Generally these vessels are offered for sale at a very low price, sometimes even given away.

The Peking

When the Dutch tug *Utrecht* arrived off Staten Island, on July 22, 1975, with her tow, *Peking,* the fact that there was no great welcoming committee was more symbolic than most people realized. The great square-rigged barque had followed the same harrowing course that had been taken by millions of others who came to the New World to find a home when they had been rejected every place else. The city where the ship had been built said she was now in too poor a condition to preserve, and the community that had her as a maritime landmark and school for over forty years could no longer support her. The *Peking* came to New York, as did so many other immigrants before her, to enter the "Golden Door" and find a future.

The American tugs of the McAllister fleet took her in tow from the *Utrecht,* the first of many helping hands that would be offered by a long list of leaders in the maritime community and thousands of everyday people, who would give time and money to the project. During the next four months, people would often come to me, knowing my interest in ships, to report that there was a real old sailing ship reposing in a Staten Island yard. She was first docked at the Pouch Terminal, a temporary home, courtesy of Tim Pouch, the owner, and one of the many friends of the South Street Seaport Museum, who now also became the friend of *Peking*. Seaport volunteers acted as watchmen as she was prepared for her last voyage.

In August of 1975, tugs of the Turecamo fleet moved the barque to the Brewers Drydock on the west shore of Staten Island. Here the ship had her hull, yards, and other steel work sandblasted. The Banks Rigging Co., a firm that gave technical and financial support to the project, installed the original foreyard,

The four-masted barque *Peking* comes to the South Street Seaport Museum, and like immigrants of the past salutes the Statue of Liberty on the way to her new home.

fore lower topsail, and jigger gaff, all of which had been removed and stored on the main deck during the Atlantic crossing.

The great success of the "Flying P Line" of Ferdinand Laeisz, of Germany, in which the *Peking* had sailed for twenty years, was due to the captains, who were not only master mariners in sail but also astute business managers. After the J. Aron Charitable Foundation bought the *Peking* in October of 1974, it started to look for an experienced captain in sail who could act as over-all business manager for the project—not an easy man to find in twentieth century America. But the foundation people were most fortunate in hiring Commander H. A. (Hap) Paulson, Jr., USCG (Ret.) for the job. Hap Paulson was the first captain of the Coast Guard Barque *Eagle* (ex-*Horst Wessel*) to have trained aboard that ship while a cadet at the Coast Guard Academy, and went on to become her master from 1968 until 1972. A major part of the *Peking* project had been the shipyard work, both here and in England, and Hap Paulson's experience with the American barque proved invaluable.

I sailed down the harbor on November 22, 1975 aboard the RV *Pisces*, a schoolboat operated by New York City for high school students studying maritime trades. It acted, for the day, as a press boat for the South Street Seaport Museum. We went to meet the *Peking* and escort her to her new home at the Museum on the East River. The twenty photographers and reporters aboard the sixty-five-foot former Army T boat saw the *Peking* for the first time as she came out of the Kill Van Kull, Staten Island waterway, nudged gently along by two Turecamo tugs, past Robin Reef Lighthouse.

This was her official entrance into the port that was to be her new home, and a city fireboat covered the sky with the traditional welcoming spray. The *Peking*'s hull and masts sparkled with a new coat of paint. She proudly displayed the colors of the International Signal flags and the pennants and burgees of the various private and government agencies that had helped to bring her this far. She sailed along, as if independent of the tugs, past the Statue of Liberty and Ellis Island, as so many other immigrants of the past had done. Passing ferries, tugs, and ships dipped their ensigns and blew whistles and horns in the traditional maritime salute.

The ship is now a permanent maritime landmark in the East River, one of the reminders that South Street is indeed a maritime museum. She has all of her standing rigging in place, and is open to the public. Many of the changes made when the *Peking* was used as a stationary schoolship at the Shaftsbury School of England have been put back to the original form. Visitors can learn about the work of a sailing ship in viewing the exhibition *"Peking and the Age of Steel Square Riggers: 1885 to 1957."* The *Peking* is one of the major examples of ship preservation in the port and is the flagship of the South Street Seaport Musem's fleet.

Musicbarge Ltd.

Across the East River, opposite the *Peking,* is a more modest example of maritime preservation, a former Erie Lackawanna, 102-foot steel barge that has found a second career. It's called Music-barge Ltd. and is now used for concerts of chamber music instead of hauling coffee. The water-borne music hall did not come easily, as is witnessed by the story of her owner and official "captain," Olga Bloom.

Olga and her husband Tobias Bloom, a violinist who played under Toscannini, would often have their musician friends come to their home to play chamber music. Mrs. Bloom recalls, " . . . what a waste, all this fine music and no audience." After her

A former coffee barge tied at the foot of Fulton Street, Brooklyn, is now a concert hall where one can hear "uncompromising music."

Ms. Olga Bloom, ''Captain'' of Bargemusic Ltd.

husband died, she had a dream that she was to provide a place for people to play what she calls ''uncompromising music.'' She first tried two wooden barges, but they were unsatisfactory. Then she found the barge of her dreams.

The reality of being a boatowner reached Mrs. Bloom when she found that converting her $10,000 bargain took all the money she made playing in Broadway shows and teaching music. She did most of the interior work herself, while others did the more specialized work, such as welding, mostly as unpaid volunteers. The interior of the barge is not just ordinary wood paneling, but mahogany, saved from a former Staten Island ferryboat that had been scrapped in 1963. The owner of the boatyard in Rockaway Beach, New York, who helped Olga Bloom find the barge, gave her a teak door, reputed to be from Kaiser Wilhelm's yacht, along with some leaded glass windows from another yacht, to help complete the nautical interior. After most of the work was done, the barge found a new home at a dock at the foot of Fulton Street, in Brooklyn, near the tower of the Great Bridge. From time to time, Olga Bloom has problems meeting the standards and codes of the city, but she has received grants and has a list of patrons who subscribe generously to Musicbarge Ltd.

Restaurants Afloat

Sharing the waterfront at the foot of Fulton Street is another barge. This one has been saved to serve again as a plush restaurant, The River Cafe. Like Olga Bloom, Buzzy O'Keefe had to navigate a sea of red tape over a fourteen-year period to get official permission to use the barge as a restaurant. It was necessary to spend some $600,000 to convert the 30 × 90-foot barge, build shoreside kitchen facilities, and clear an area for parking.

The original idea was to have the dining area on a floating barge. This proved impractical so the barge is now supported in the water on piles, holding stationary even with the changing tides.

The entrance to the restaurant is through an outdoor cafe, passing into a building that houses a reception room and kitchen, and then down a gangway to the dining area and bar on the barge. The water side of the barge has been enclosed in glass and offers one of the most spectacular views of the lower Manhattan skyline and harbor, including the Statue of Liberty. The East River still has heavy marine traffic, especially small boats, and there is a constant parade of tugs, small tankers, and barges, and an occasional deep-water vessel for diners to watch. Almost the only problem with the River Cafe, now, is the expensive menu.

The *Chauncey M. Depew* has also found a second career as a restaurant, although she first sailed many miles from the time she was built in 1913, at Bath, Maine, until she became another fixed maritime landmark in the port. Starting life as the *Rangeley,* for eleven years after her launching, the 185-foot long, 652-ton vessel ran in Maine waters for the Maine Central Railroad, out of Bar Harbor. She was taken over by the government during World War I.

When peace came, the eleven-hundred passenger boat was sold to the famous Hudson River Dayline fleet. She did well in the excursion business on the river, taking the overflow from larger boats. At the outbreak of World War II, the *Chauncey M.*

Above: The River Cafe, a dining room on an old barge, mounted on piles in the East River. *Below:* The *Chauncey M. Depew,* stationed in the New Jersey meadowlands, is one of the lucky boats that have found a second career. A veteran of World Wars I and II, plus a career in Bermuda and on the Hudson River, the well-known *Depew* is now a Supper Club.

Depew was again called to serve, and the War Shipping Administration took away her name and gave her the unglamorous number FS-89.

After the war, the ship again went into the excursion business under her old name, this time in the Chesapeake Bay area, running between Baltimore and Tolchester, Maryland. In 1950, the government of Bermuda bought the boat, and for the next twenty years she sailed the island's green waters as a tender, taking passengers from cruise ships to the shore. Displaced by a Diesel tender in 1969, she steamed under her own power back to the Chesapeake Bay area.

At that point, the white excursion steamer entered a period of decline, at a dock on the North East River in Maryland. Moving only vertically, with the ever changing tides, the *Chauncey M. Depew* came to grief in 1971 when an inlet valve froze and split, letting in the river, tipping her over to sink at the dock. The boat spent almost two years on the bottom before she was refloated and saved. There was talk of sending her back to her native Maine, but instead she ended up on the Hudson River, in the port.

In the spring of 1977, two tugs of the Bronx Towing Company took the sixty-four-year old *Chauncey M. Depew* in hand for a trip to her new home in the Hackensack River, at Secaucus. She is now the Aratusa Supper Club, minus her steam engine, lifeboats, and any rigging but a string of lights. Senator Chauncey M. Depew, whose name she carried, was said to be one of the greatest after-dinner speakers the Republican party ever produced. He would feel right at home boarding his namesake, entering the rooms decorated in turn-of-the-century style from the canopied gangway, and casting his eye over the expensive menu.

On Monday, April 3, 1905, the steam ferryboat *Binghamton* first entered scheduled trans-Hudson River service between Hoboken and Barclay Street in lower Manhattan. Mr. Harry Cotterell, a ferryboat buff and historian, notes that at this time there were some forty-eight different ferry routes crossing the harbor waters. Today there are only three active ferry lines left in the port: Staten Island, Governors Island, and Hart Island.

The *Binghamton* sailed back and forth across the Hudson until the bridges and tunnels took away the traffic. On November 22, 1967, the then Erie-Lackawanna Railroad shut down the service, the last ferry operation anywhere on the Hudson River. It is estimated that the *Binghamton* had carried a hundred and twenty-

The *Binghamton*, while still carrying passengers across the Hudson in her first
life.

five million people, traveling over two hundred thousand miles, but never leaving the river.

At that time, there wasn't much of a market for a 1,462 gross-ton ferry that could carry 1,986 passengers and twenty-eight vehicles. After two years, however, a group of investors did buy the boat and start the long voyage through the stormy waters of financing and red tape that would turn her into a restaurant. It took from 1969 to 1975 before the *Binghamton* was first opened to the public. During that time there was a change in ownership and a take-over by a bank for non-payment of loans. The new owners were encouraged to continue converting the ferryboat by the Edgewater, New Jersey, Borough Council, which gave them mooring rights and parking for four hundred cars on the waterfront, off River Road, three miles south of the George Washington Bridge.

The conversion to a restaurant entailed keeping as much of the original vessel as possible, yet providing the necessary equipment and space needed for the daily operations. As an example, the two coal-fired steam boilers were removed to make room for a kitchen, but one of the two steam-compound engines remains as a focal point in a lower dining room. Most of the exterior changes on the boat have been made to return it to its original state at launching in 1905. She is now, smokestack included, in a white livery, the way she was until the railroad changed her colors to an undistinguished tan and white in 1920. Built as a double-ender, so she could be loaded and unloaded without turning around, the *Binghamton* now has both ends enclosed with picture windows.

The ferryboat is a moderately priced restaurant, with entertainment at night. For the young, a visit to the *Binghamton* offers a taste of an era they never knew. For those who remember the days of the railroad ferries on the Hudson River, she offers a chance to sail back in time.

The Annie C. Ross

When the great American square-riggers disappeared from the world's oceans at the turn of the century, victims of the battle with steam and motor-driven ships, there was still enough profit left for the operation of wind-driven, schooner-rigged vessels. They were launched from the shipyards of Maine as late as the 1920s for commercial service. The number of schooners in this period actually increased, built with more tonnage, more masts (the *Thomas W. Lawson* held the record with seven), and power hoisting machinery to turn capstans and windlasses, enabling them to sail with smaller crews. These schooners sailed into the twentieth century, not because of any romantic attachment to sail, but because on a small investment and with low operating costs—which unfortunately meant low wages and poor food for the crew—efficient owners and operators made a fine profit.

The economics of the power vessels finally won out after World War I, for wasn't the oil needed to fire the boilers, or fuel the Diesel engines so cheap that operators could afford to turn from the free winds? The last of the schooners furled their sails, and after four hundred years of commercial use, wind-driven vessels faded from the seas. They had made a valiant fight, being run down at night by fast steamships and driven ashore by the Great Depression.

The schooners retreated to join the hulks of the square-riggers in the back waters of the great ports they had served so long, and to die a silent death, for wooden ships have no scrap value. It is still possible to see some of the old hulks today, at a place called Port Johnson, on Kill Van Kull, off the New Jersey shore. Sail would now be used only for recreational boats and racing yachts. The traditional horseshoes, nailed to so many of the schooners' sampson posts, had lost their good luck charm.

One of the last schooners to call at the Port of New York and New Jersey and have it as her homeport was the four-master *Annie C. Ross*. She has earned a place in American maritime history, not for any spectacular rig or deeds, merely for the fact that she was one of the last wind-driven ships operated on the East Coast in commercial service. She is also well remembered because there are still sailormen around who crewed aboard her during her last days.

The *Annie C. Ross* was launched in 1917, named for the wife of her first captain, and built to fill the wartime need for cargo carriers. She came from the shipyard of Percy & Small, of Bath, Maine, a yard noted for building fine wooden vessels, even into the 1920s. The shipyard is now part of the Bath Marine Museum. She was a beautiful sight when she slid down the ways with a white hull and flags flying from her four masts. She first entered the coal-carrying trade, but could not compete with steamers, so she became a lumber carrier, a service in which she stayed for the remainder of her commercial days. She was 175 feet, six inches overall, with a 38-foot beam, and weighed 791 gross tons—small

The *Star of the Sea*, former cargo schooner *Annie C. Ross*, found a new home on the East River as a training ship for the Catholic Sea Cadets.

enough to be loaded aboard one of today's container ships.

The lumber trade for schooners centered around George-town, South Carolina, the southern loading port, and the storage yards on Newtown Creek, in Maspeth, Queens, on the East River, still a home for lumber yards. Sailing in this trade, the *Annie C. Ross* made the round trip from New York to Georgetown and return in as few as twenty days, including the loading and unloading of up to 700,000 board feet of lumber.

In the 1930s, the ownership of the boat changed from Captain Alex Ross to Captain Joseph Zuljevic of Bay Ridge, Brooklyn, and she continued coming to New York in the lumber trade. The four-master sailed with a crew of seven: captain, two mates, three able seamen, and a cook. There was no radio, and in the days before radar and Loran, the skill of the master navigated and piloted the *Annie C. Ross* up and down the coast and into harbors, with only the assistance of a tug for docking. A ''make or break'' donkey gasoline engine helped raise the anchor. Without refrigeration, crew memberes lived on salt ''horse'' meat and canned food, with the cook also helping to tend the sails. (One cook went ashore and found his rigging skills were in greater demand than his cooking skills.) Yachtsmen who would visit the vessel would marvel at the size of the crew in light of the weight and size of the gear.

While the *Annie C. Ross* sailed the coast and the years passed, the sailormen started to fade from the waterfront, with the old schooners outlasting many of them. The low pay, poor food, and hard work did not draw many young men into the boats. In the late 1930s, Black Charlie, who was the last shipping master for wind-driven vessels in the port, had difficulty finding experienced hands to crew the schooners. The legion of aging men, mostly Norwegians and Finns, with no home but the sea, became fewer at the old Seaman's Church Institute at 25 South Street, and in the cheap hotels of the city's Bowery.

We are fortunate that toward the last working days of the *Annie C. Ross*, members of a new breed came aboard to learn the ropes, and they are still around to relate their experiences. Most of these sailed as ''workaways,'' comparable to today's interns in many professions, on vacation from school and happy without pay just to be part of a real, commercial sailing ship's crew. Unlike the true sailormen, in later days they left the schoonerman's life, but they never forgot their experiences under sail in the coastwise trade.

In November of 1940, the *Annie C. Ross* brought a cargo of

lumber from Georgetown to Newtown Creek and went into a period of temporary lay-up, a term that often spelled the end of a vessel's sailing days. She became a maritime landmark, the four masts visible from the then new Kosciusko Bridge over the Creek. Unlike the first World War, World War II offered no demand for the schooner, and as the years passed, her paint peeled and her rigging sagged and frayed.

In 1947 it looked as if she would again leave the Creek, when Captain Joseph Rosario bought her. He started to make plans to return the schooner to the Cape Verde Island trade, one of the last passenger services left in the world to cross the Atlantic under sail. Her topmasts were lowered to fit under the bridge in order to sail out into the East River, but the good captain died before his dream was to become a reality. Frank O. Braynard, one of the founders of the South Street Seaport Museum, and a dreamer who gave the city Op-Sail '76, appreciated the *Annie C. Ross's* historical value and started to raise money to have her rerigged to sail in the harbor for National Maritime Day. Bethlehem Steel agreed to do the job, gratis, but by this time, the vessel was so in debt that if she left the Creek she would not be permitted to return.

The boat was next sold at auction, for her debts, to an actor, Scott Moore, who lived aboard. He had a new plan, one of the more unusual ones for a second career for an old ship. He wanted to turn her into a seagoing TV studio. Moore continued to live aboard the schooner, but his plan never materialized.

In 1954, the Catholic Sea Scouts bought the old schooner for two thousand dollars, had her towed to the east side of Manhattan, to a pier at the foot of 26th Street. Her name was changed to *Star of the Sea,* and the scouts painted "training ship" on her bow. Her rig was changed by removing the top masts, and she now became what schoonermen termed a "bald header." She stayed at the Manhattan pier for a time, with the scouts rowing around her in lifeboats and dreaming of the day they would take her back to sea under sail. They proved their intention of sailing the old schooner again when they had her towed from the city pier to Hempstead Bay, in Long Island Sound. The plan was to have the boys carry on the needed work while the vessel swung at anchor. On September 2, the young crew of nine scouts discovered that there was water coming in through the rotting hull timbers. She was off Morgan's Point Bark breakwater, at Glen Cove, Long Island.

In the finest tradition of the sea, a young crew member reversed the national ensign to signal distress, and the U.S. Coast Guard and Nassau County Marine Police came to their aid with handy billy pumps. In the three days that followed the pumps lost the battle and the sea took command on September 5, 1955, forcing the crew to abandon ship. Just before they left the old schooner, one of the boys took down the American flag, ending her thirty-eight years of sailing under the stars and stripes. She sank in twenty-one feet of water, and since the vessel had a draft of eighteen feet, she was a sorry sight with her four masts sticking out of the water.

On September 6, looters went aboard the half-sunken schooner and stole her steering wheel and lanterns. High winds took down two masts, and the other two were removed in an aborted attempt to raise her. The wreck soon became a menace to navigation in the busy harbor, and in the spring of 1956 the Army Engineers awarded an $11,900 contract. This money, that would have meant so much a short time before in refitting the schooner for the sea, was now used for her removal. The firm of Edward O. Sanches, of New Bedford, received the contract to tow the *Annie C. Ross* to ninety feet of water and sink her. The last four-master ended her days buried at sea.

The Ellis Island

The ferryboat *Ellis Island* is still visible, mostly at low tide, in the slip at Ellis Island, sunk up close to the art deco terminal. The boat has lost just about all its identity, with the smokestack fallen over on a crumbling wooden deckhouse. Year after year, the derelict seems to cling to the old Immigration Station from which she received her name, and from which she provided a shuttle service to Manhattan's Battery for fifty years.

There are special reasons that place this little ferry in a distinctive class, above all others that worked the waters of the port: her unusual mission of carrying some fifteen million new Americans on the last leg of their journey through the Golden Door; the ability to provide this service, unassisted, for a period of fifty years; and, because of her steel hull, her slow death over the past thirty-plus years rather than a voyage to the ship breakers.

When the Immigration Station was first opened in 1892, it was served by a variety of unsuitable boats, until Congress appropriated money to build a ferry. The contract was awarded to Harlan & Hollingsworth, of Wilmington, Delaware, a firm that

175

built most of the ferries in New York. The boat was designed along the lines of the Jersey Central Railroad ferries. She was launched on March 18, 1904, and carried the champagne bottle used to christen her in a display cabinet throughout her long career.

Although the boat followed traditional lines for a ferry, she was unlike other such vessels in that the lower deck was used only for passengers and baggage, since there were no provisions for vehicles on Ellis Island. It was also unique in having a sick bay and a special padded cell for violent mental patients from the hospital on the island. The commissioner of immigrations had a special cabin for his use when aboard.

The boat was built at a cost of $105,000, with a special steel hull to withstand the dangers of ice floes in the harbor. The upper structure was wood, with one high funnel amidship. She was 106 feet long, 37 feet wide, with a draft of 9 feet, 3 inches and a displacement of 660 tons. The power plant was 450 horsepower, generated by a compound steam engine fed from two hand-fired, coal Scotch Marine boilers. As was common with all ferryboats, she had screw propellers on each end to eliminate turning around.

The little ferry made the round trip from the island to the Battery and back between the hours of six A.M. and midnight, taking fifteen minutes, including loading and unloading. She was in continual service except twice a year for the annual dry-docking and Coast Guard inspection. The one-boat service caused many hardships when she had to be removed for emergency repairs. A new Diesel boat was authorized at a cost of $500,000 in 1940, but died on the drawing board due to World War II.

The procedure for immigrants landing in the U.S. called for the steamship companies to transport them from their piers to Ellis Island on barges. When they boarded the *Ellis Island* ferryboat, their immigration ordeal was over and the mile and a half trip across the waters of the upper bay brought an end to their Old World life. Often the desire to assimilate into the mainstream of their new life was so great that relatives would go over to the island with "American clothes," and they would change on the ferry, discarding the last traces of their old homes. The few immigrants who were rejected out of the thousands that came over would never sail on the *Ellis Island*, but be taken back to the pier by the steamship company, to be returned to the land of their origin. At the height of the immigration wave, the little ferry carried some 2,500,000 passengers annually.

Although the *Ellis Island* had a short run, she operated in one of the busiest sections of New York Harbor. Running on a tight schedule during the years of peak traffic, the vessel occasionally suffered propeller and rudder damage, and some minor collisions with barges. Even today conflicting currents of the East and Hudson rivers at the Battery make the Manhattan landing a difficult one. Whenever the ferry had mechanical difficulty, she would still have to limp along until a replacement could be found.

One of the saddest episodes in her career happened in September of 1913. A railing on the boat had been damaged by another boat while she was docked at the barge office in Manhattan. Repairs gave way while the ferry was steaming ahead, dumping five passengers overboard. A civilian contractor's employee was killed by the ship's propeller and an Immigration Service Inspector died from drowning in the accident.

The most dramatic incident in the history of Ellis Island, and in the life of the ferry, happened on July 30, 1916, when the infamous Black Tom Wharf, on the New Jersey shore, less than a mile from the island, exploded. This disaster was thought to be the work of German saboteurs trying to stop the shipment of munitions to the Allies. Barges filled with ammunition broke loose, drifted across the water, and set fire to the seawall. Ellis Island was saved from total destruction by a tugboat crew that towed the barges away before they exploded. Terrified immigrants, mindful of the war in Europe at the time, were evacuated to Manhattan on the *Ellis Island*.

Ellis Island closed its doors on November 12, 1954. The ferry operated until November 29, 1954, when it made its last run from the Battery with one of her veteran skippers, Captain Ives of Lynbrook, Long Island, in command. A Norwegian merchant seaman who had missed his ship was the last passenger the ferry transported, out of an estimated twenty million. She tied up at the slip at Ellis Island and after fifty years of faithful service, her "Finished with Engines" was rung up on the engine telegraph for the last time. It was said the boat logged over a million miles in the span of her career, never once leaving New York Harbor.

The ferry was offered for sale as part of the package with the island. During the next fourteen years she only moved vertically with the tides, until the weekend of August 10, 1968. As if she could no longer live alone at the deserted island, she sank from neglect. Divers found a hole in the steel hull, and she lay on the bottom with a 20° list in the shallow water. Now the harbor water washed through the boat while the weather and seasons took a toll on the deckhouse above water.

Investigation proved it would be too expensive to salvage the historic ferryboat and it was recommended that a contract be let for demolition, a job that was never bid. As if trying to cling to the past at the island she served so long, the *Ellis Island* remained at the slip she had known for more than eighty years after she was launched. I would look for her any time I was near the island and noted when her stack fell down and crashed into what was left of the deckhouse. Today the boat is nothing but part of the memory of those who sailed aboard her into a new life.

The Alexander Hamilton

Maritime preservation is not all success stories, and one of the saddest failures is the saga of the Hudson River Dayliner, the *Alexander Hamilton*. Steamboating on the Hudson River started in 1807, with Robert Fulton's *Clermont,* and ended in 1971, when the *Alexander Hamilton* was taken out of service. She had sailed the river for forty-seven seasons, carrying up to four thousand passengers between New York City and Albany. With two side-mounted paddle wheels, powered by a 3,400 horsepower and inclined, reciprocating steam engine, she was the last of her breed. With the Hudson's beautiful shores as a backdrop, and with her white superstructure, tall twin smokestacks, and flags flying from ten staffs, she was a majestic sight.

The 2,367 gross-ton steamboat was taken out of service by the Day Line because of the high cost of fuel and the expense of her fifty-man crew. She was replaced for the 1972 season by a new Diesel-powered boat, the *Dayliner,* which is still in service. Everyone was positive the excursion boat would start a second career in the newly formed South Street Seaport Museum as a restaurant, and she was towed around to the East River's Pier 15. It soon became evident that the struggling museum could not finance so large a project, and for security reasons the excursion boat was moved across the East River to the old Brooklyn Navy Yard. When she was again moved to the Hudson River and laid up at Harborside Terminal in Jersey City her future started to look dim.

The Railroad Pier Company of Middletown Township, New Jersey, became her next owner, and in 1974 the *Hamilton* was towed to Atlantic Highlands, still with the idea of conversion to a restaurant. While the vessel was in Atlantic Highlands, vandals pierced her hull and she settled on a mudbank. A group of former crew members and steamboat buffs then formed the Alexander

The *Alexander Hamilton* sits high and dry at Atlantic Highlands, New Jersey, where vandals pierced her hull and she settled on a mud bank.

Hamilton Preservation Society and had the boat accepted by the state as an Historic Site. The Preservation Society went on, in April of 1977, to have the *Hamilton* placed on the National Register of Historic Places, joining some seven hundred other sites and objects in the country, and striving for financial security for the venture with eligibility for Federal funds and matching grants that never materialized.

The Railroad Pier Co. underestimated the cost of conversion, gave up its plan, and sold the *Alexander Hamilton* to Sulko Pier Enterprises, Ltd, Poughkeepsie, New York, which, like all the others, planned on returning the boat to the Hudson River as a restaurant and museum. After some months of failure, the new owners, who had paid $200,000 for the vessel, finally refloated her on September 15, 1977. The future once again looked bright for the *Alexander Hamilton*.

The Coast Guard wanted to inspect the boat before it could give permission to tow the old girl through New York Harbor and up to her new home on the Hudson River. It was planned to tow the boat to Weehawken for additional repairs before taking her up the Hudson. The U.S. Navy, in a move that it would come to regret, allowed the *Alexander Hamilton* to be tied up at its weapons pier in Earle, Leonardo, New Jersey.

There are conflicting accounts of what happened to the *Alexander Hamilton* on the night of November 7, 1977, while tied up to the Navy pier. A storm came out of the northeast, bringing high waves, strong winds, and seven inches of rain across Sandy Hook Bay. Some say that the pumps aboard the old excursion boat could not keep up with the seas coming in. Others say that a barge struck the boat, or that she got hung up on the pier, tilting over and taking on water. In any event, the *Alexander Hamilton* sank in sixteen feet of water that night at Leonardo.

Today there is little left of her; all the wooden superstructure has long since been carried away, along with the pilothouse, and only the skeleton of steel remains. The matter of what to do with the once queen of the Hudson River is being debated in Federal Court, with the U.S. Navy trying to have the derelict removed and Sulko Pier Enterprises maintaining that because the vessel is on the National Register of Historic Places, the government should provide salvage. The *Alexander Hamilton* is a classic example of the frustration and failure of many well-meaning people.

The steam excursion boat *City of Keansburg* waits at a pier in New Jersey City, on the Hudson River, for a second career that may never come.

The City of Keansburg

Like the *Chauncey M. Depew* and the *Alexander Hamilton*, the *City of Keansburg* was part of the great excursion boat fleet that once sailed the waters of the port. She was built at Newburg, New York, the last boat to come down the ways of the Marvel Company shipyard in 1926. The 1,037 gross ton vessel, with distinctive twin smokestacks, was powered by two sets of 750 horsepower three-cylinder triple expansion steam engines, and had a passenger capacity of 2,036. For years the *City of Keansburg* operated from Pier A and Battery Park, at the tip of Manhattan, making three round trips a day to Keansburg, New Jersey. In the evenings the boat would sail the harbor on moonlight cruises, and her large dance floor was a favorite attraction. When the pier at Atlantic Highlands was destroyed by fire in 1965, the *City of*

Keansburg tried to pay her way by running two harbor cruises a day from the Battery, but in 1968, the boat was placed in lay-up.

The *City of Keansburg* then started a familiar voyage, going on to City Island in the Bronx, where new owners planned on turning her into a floating restaurant. She wallowed there for years, then returned to the Hudson to be tied up in the McAllister's shipyard in New Jersey and put up for sale. Each year a boat is out of service she gets nearer to the end of her days. The shipyard is now fighting a court order to be moved out of Jersey City, and there are no announced plans for the classic steam excursion boat.

USS *Intrepid*

Military vessels have found an easier voyage to a second career, but many others that saw wartime service never again made the transition back to peacetime work.

Since June of 1982 the aircraft carrier USS *Intrepid* has dominated the west side waterfront of Manhattan. Launched from the Newport News Shipyard in Virginia, just days before Pearl Harbor, the *Intrepid* went on to serve the nation through the Vietnam conflict. She also served twice as the prime recovery ship for the space program. The veteran carrier has credit for her aircraft groups sinking and damaging two hundred eighty-nine enemy ships, including the battleship *Yamato*. She, in turn, was hit by Kamikaze attacks and lost over two hundred airmen and one hundred crew members.

Under president James R. Ean, the Intrepid Musuem Foundation was created, in 1978, to bring the historic carrier to New York as a Sea-Air-Space Museum. While the 900-foot carrier waited in the Philadelphia Navy Yard, the foundation received support from the City of New York, floated bonds, and received dockage at Pier 86-South for permanent berthing in Manhattan. As part of the city's renaissance of the waterfront, over two million dollars was loaned for the restoration of the pier and provision of safe moorage for the aircraft carrier. The total cost for the conversion of the carrier to a stationary museum ran to $22 million, of which $14.2 million came from tax-exempt bonds issued by the Foundation.

On an overcast day, June 13, 1982, the USS *Intrepid* entered the upper bay of New York Harbor and was towed to her new berth on the West side of Manhattan, at Forty-sixty Street. Seeing her from aboard the USCGC *Raritan*, a small harbor tug that was also a veteran of World War II, I couldn't help but feel that the USS *Intrepid* was one of the most successful maritime restorations the port has yet seen. Tourists flocked to the new museum, especially former crew members who wanted to show their families the ship on which they had served in one of the wars in which she had fought. Recently, however, the museum has found out what most groups have learned who have taken on the preservation of a large ship: that it takes a continual infusion of money to keep the project on an even keel. Attendance fell off in the cold weather, and the cost of heating such a large space eats into the operating budget. Only time will tell how successful the USS *Intrepid* Foundation will be as the veteran carrier fights one of her most difficult battles to survive.

The SS *New Bedford*

Although much smaller than the USS *Intrepid* the SS *New Bedford* also saw combat duty in World War II. She started life in 1928, one of the "sound steamers" that sailed for the New Bedford, Wood's Hole, Martha's Vineyard, and Nantucket Steamboat Line, which sums up her operating waters. The 202-foot long vessel carried cars and passengers to the islands, and with a shallow draft of thirteen feet, she fit nicely into the waters of Buzzards Bay and Nantucket Sound.

In 1942 there was an acute shortage of bottoms, especially vessels that could serve in shallow harbors for the planned invasion of France. The *New Bedford* was taken over by the British Ministry of War Transportation and painted gray. Her open decks were covered with thick wood planking and fitted with two small caliber deck guns, before she sailed in convoy across the Atlantic. She no longer looked like an excursion boat, but like a ship of war.

Crewed by British volunteers, the *New Bedford* joined convoy RB-1, a fleet of converted sound steamers from New England and the Chesapeake Bay area, vessels that were never designed or built to sail across the Atlantic. On the fifth day out of Boston, the U-boats hit the convoy, sinking some of the excursion ferries and an escort. After the sixth day of attack, there was no convoy and the *New Bedford* made a run, alone, to the nearest English port, helped by a storm that gave cover with heavy rains. She was converted to a hospital ship, once again in her white peacetime livery, with a green band and a large red cross on each side

The *New Bedford,* dying a slow death at Witte's Salvage Yard in Rossville, Staten Island.

and on her stack. She went into Omaha Beach on June 6, 1944, in some of the heaviest fighting of the invasion, and survived without incident, going on to shuttle troops between Southampton and LeHavre.

At eighteen years of age, the *New Bedford* once again sailed the Atlantic in order to return to her home in 1946. In 1947 she found new employment when purchased from the government by the Sound Steamship Lines for service as a ferry again, between Providence, Rhode Island and Block Island, in Long Island Sound. By 1955 the company no longer needed the *New Bedford,* and she was put in lay-up. Still unemployed, the steamer went to New York Harbor where her owners looked for work for her while she was docked at an unused pier in New Jersey.

By 1967, the owners were happy to agree upon the price of

$3,005 for the *New Bedford,* and she made her last voyage to the Witte's Marine Salvage Corporation yard on the west shore of Staten Island, New York at Rossville, on the Arthur Kill waterway. Here at Witte's, which is like a marine version of the fabled elephants' burial ground, *New Bedford* joined the fleet of old tugs, barges, military craft, small tankers, and ferryboats that made this their last port of call.

The John W. Brown

Over the period of thirty-seven years just about everyone who lived in or traveled to New York City saw the Liberty ship *John W. Brown* tied up at her pier, first on Manhattan's east side and then in 1964, at Pier 42 on the Hudson River. She had become a maritime landmark in the city, a stationary schoolship, a floating high school for students interested in the maritime trades. The *John W. Brown* left the Port of New York and New Jersey in July of 1983, towed to the James River Reserve fleet of the U.S. Maritime Administration, and she now waits for a new lease on life as a museum.

The *Brown* was built at Baltimore, Maryland, by the Bethlehem Fairfield shipyard, the same yard that built the first of the war-time Liberty ships, the *Patrick Henry.* The *Brown* was built in forty-one days, named after an American labor leader of West Coast carpenters, and launched on September 7, 1942. She was just one of some 2,700 Liberty ships built for World War II, and today is one of two such ships left. (The second ship is the *Jeremiah O'Brien,* which is preserved at the Port of San Francisco,

The Liberty Ship *John W. Brown* in Wartime Livery

California, and sails once a year for National Maritime Day in May.)

The *Brown* started life as a general break-bulk cargo carrier, but then as the wartime needs arose she was converted to a limited capacity troop carrier. This conversion made her a perfect schoolship after the war. The ship's wartime exploits were not very spectacular, considering the service of the Liberties as a whole on the North Atlantic, or the Murmansk run to Russia and the great invasion on D-day at Normandy beaches. The ship did, however, see combat in the Mediterranean at the invasion of Anzio. She was a lucky ship, unlike the 195 of her sisters that were lost to enemy action and other casualties of war.

After the war most of the Liberty ships were sold off to foreign buyers, or placed in mothballs in the reserve fleet. In the passing years they left the National Defense Reserve Fleet to make their last voyage to the ship breakers' yard, or to be sunk off the coast as man-made fish reefs. The *Brown* again was lucky, after having a brief career as a civilian carrier for the States Marine Lines, she came to New York City in 1946. The Federal Government loaned the ship to the New York City Board of Education for use as a stationary schoolship to train students on the high school level in the basic maritime trades for careers at sea. At this time the *Brown* was a welcome replacement for the aging ferryboat *Brooklyn*, which had been used by the Board of Education as a schoolship since the late thirties.

The design for the Liberty ships came from the prototype of a British tramp steamer, dating from 1879, and updated by the famous New York naval architects Gibbs & Cox. These standard ships were called "ugly ducklings," by President Franklin D. Roosevelt. They were simple to build by unskilled wartime shipyard workers, who included many women, and easily manned and sailed off to the sea war by quickly-trained crews of civilian volunteers, including some as young as sixteen years of age. Parts of the ship were built by subcontractors with no experience in marine work. A stove company built lifeboats, and the bed plats for the main steam engines were made by a firm, that in peace time, turned out gravestones.

Over the years the *Brown* served as a schoolship for generations of students, including girls in the later years, who learned the ropes of the seafaring trades. Many went on to maritime colleges or joined the Coast Guard and U.S. Navy for careers at sea. By 1982, because of the small number of American merchant ships, there was little demand for graduates of the *Brown*, and

Schoolship SS *John W. Brown*

the Board of Education elected to move the maritime program to a building ashore. In July of 1983, the *John W. Brown* was towed from the Hudson River by a Moran tug for the Reserve Fleet in the James River, Virginia. The Maritime Administration at this writing is looking for a group to take over the ship as a museum, and many old salts hope that the *Brown* might be returned to the Port of New York and New Jersey. Perhaps the *John W. Brown* will continue to be a lucky ship.

Witte's Marine Grave Yard

The ghost fleet at Witte's has more history of the Port of New York & New Jersey than any museum. It's possible to see the changes in marine propulsion with all the old steamboats and ferries, and, later, even some of the older Diesel vessels too. The once proud ferryboats that were displaced over the years by bridges and tunnels have come to rest here. Many of the small military boats, which could never make it in the civilian market,

187

are tied together with the barges that were displaced by container ships in the port.

While fires over the years have removed the wooden vessels, salable parts are slowly sold off the rest of the vessels. Witte's Marine Salvage yard holds all the vessels that will never have a second career, now that their sailing days are over. They are condemned to a slow death with the ever changing tides, seasons, and weather. Don't plan on visiting Witte's, for you'll receive no welcome there—especially from the junk yard dogs.

Witte's Salvage Yard, the last port of call for steam tugs, ferryboats, World War II Navy boats, and old barges.

X   THE SHIP and HARBOR ENTHUSIASTS   W.H.M.

THE LAST HOORAH of the inner Port was in the fifties. Then, as the transatlantic liners began to disappear, freighter companies shifted to container docks in New Jersey. The Manhattan waterfront grew increasingly desolate and lonely. This, however, ignited interest in the history of New York Harbor and its diverse, far-flung operations. Preservation projects, specialty magazines and newsletters, walking tours, photographic small-boat cruises, and monthly lectures on salty topics began to be developed. But as their subscription and membership lists gradually increased, general interest in the Port began to fade. In the fifties, for example, major newspapers had full pages devoted to maritime affairs as well as daily shipping schedules. Within a decade, however, the appearance of articles, and even schedules, became sporadic: a spread of photos on the last sailing of the *Queen Mary,* the demise by fire of a West Side pier, and the "open house" on a visiting naval vessel were among the occasional features. By 1984, when a new cruise ship first arrived, there wasn't even a mention.

In the midst of realizations that the Port was indeed changing, and changing very rapidly, many wanted to overcome the emptiness and decay that was setting in. Assuredly, the most ambitious project to date has been the South Street Seaport development, situated on the East River shore of Lower Manhattan. It began in the mid-sixties, just as the shipping and adjacent fishing industries in that area began to fade. While the covered piers offered little of interest, the surrounding neighborhood was of tremendous intrinsic value, and architecturally charming: charismatic warehouses, Federal style row buildings, narrow streets and lanes in the shadows of the towers of the financial district. Frank O. Braynard, then the public relations director of the Moran Towing Company, joined the original restoration project. "Peter Sanford (the South Street president)," he wrote, wanted to preserve an entire area—several piers, seven blocks, and some one hundred old buildings, from John Street north to the Brooklyn Bridge. He wanted to create a museum complex in the true and original meaning of the word "museum." He wanted a place for the muses, a place where music, the arts, fine food, dance, good entertainment, culture, and the past could all mix and be enjoyed by great numbers of people. South Street Seaport Museum is today (1985) closer to Peter Sanford's dream, in my opinion, than even dreamer Peter ever imagined could evolve. It is a modern miracle made possible by his dedication, hard work, and fantastic guts. With the help of many wonderful people, such as his wife Norma and shipper Jakob Isbrandtsen, Peter pushed ahead against the most impossible odds and created a new and wonderful thing for all New York. The evolution of South Street Seaport Museum still has many years to go; it is far from finished. But the dream has materialized sooner and better than many thought possible. Go see it, join it, and become a member! Help it grow and expand!

For many years, the Seaport lagged. There was mismanagement, a continual lack of funds, and an overall lack of cohesiveness about the project. However, by the late seventies, the giant Rouse Corporation, master builders of inner harbor redevelopments (including Baltimore and Boston) and shopping plazas, saw the South Street area as ripe and promising for complete renewal. The results have been impressive. The "Museum" is now a combination of many things: shops, including many interesting boutiques and specialty emporiums, a diverse array of restaurants

The *Mon Lei*, built in 1855 in Fukien, China, visits New York Harbor during Operation Sail.

190

Pier 17, the South Street Seaport Complex

191

(with offerings from Coney Island-style hot dogs to Japanese sushi and French onion soup), and a multi-media spectacular entitled "The South Street Venture" that uses 150 theatrical effects, 31 screens and 104 projectors. Adjacent are several restored ships, open docks, and a full schedule of fair-weather outdoor concerts and recitals. One of the ships, the schooner *Pioneer*, offers three-hour harbor cruises in the Lower Bay. There are also special programs, particularly diverse in the peak summer months, of workshops, lectures, film series, walking tours, and special events. The Seaport is now a fine addition to New York and is definitely worth several visits.

Another city-based group passionately interested in ships and shipping has been the local branch of the World Ship Society. First formed in Britain, in 1946, and now boasting ten thousand international members, the first informal gatherings of the society among New York enthusiasts were held in the fall of 1965. A full schedule from monthly meetings to walking tours in Brooklyn and Hoboken has been in force ever since. The local branch currently has a membership of about two hundred. Richard Sand-

The annual Inernational Lifeboat Races are a typical summer event off Battery Park on July Fourth, sponsored by the Maritime Association of the Port of New York as part of the Harbor Festival Celebrations.

strom, vice-chairman of the Society, which receives its mail at the Swedish Church at 5 East 48th Street, is the enthusiastic program organizer. He writes:

> We have a group of people as members from all walks of life—writers, photographers, bankers—who have a genuine interest in ships, particularly the great ocean liners. They are among the most knowledgeable in New York about marine affairs.
>
> Our purpose has been to educate and entertain people on a variety of maritime subjects, such as tugs, freighters, and tankers. Even though ocean liners and cruise ships are of the greatest interest, we do have a well-rounded list of monthly talks and slide presentations. Hopefully, we enlighten some of our members and guests. Furthermore, we bring people together of a similar interest, where they can exchange ideas and news, and even swap memorabilia.
>
> Over the past twenty years, our programs have included lectures on the Navy, deep-sea towing, shipwrecks in the Straits of Magellan, merchant shipping in China, saving a wartime Liberty ship, and salvaging the *Andrea Doria*, as well as recollections from a Cunard captain, visits from well-known authors, and grand tours in slides of such ships as the *Queen Mary* and *Normandie*.
>
> While many of our members are from the metropolitan area, there are others from as far away as California, Arizona, and Florida. We have a monthly newsletter, which is a most important link and provides a combination of items: a monthly meeting announcement, news about shipping and New York harbor, and personal items.
>
> Periodically, we organize "outside" activities, such as group cruises on the liners *Vera Cruz* and *Britanis*, a tour of the U.S. Merchant Marine Academy at Kings Point, and of the old Brooklyn Navy Yard, and chartered harbor boat tours that sail off to the almost forgotten backwaters and inlets of New York harbor.

Similar groups, which have also organized meetings and tours and issued publications, are the local chapters of the Steamship Historical Society of America, the National Maritime Historical Society, and the Ship Lore & Model Club. The newest entry is the Ocean Liner Museum Project. Formed in 1983, and still without a permanent home at the time of writing, their mailing address is P.O. Box 232, Bowling Green Station, New York 10274. They, too, publish a newsletter, though on a quarterly basis. They have staged a gala ball, reminiscent of a grander era, aboard the liner *Rotterdam*. They have recently been awarded, among many other artifacts, the 600-pound steam whistle from the legendary *Normandie*. While planning some future exhibits, including one that highlights the fiftieth anniversary of New York's Luxury Liner

New Yorkers rediscovered the waterfront through Operation Sail, as evidenced by this large group on a West Side pier.

Row in the West Forties, the Ocean Liner Museum is seeking accommodations where photos, records, and those oversized brochures can be housed and displayed. Its trustees include authors Walter Lord, John Maxtone-Graham, and Frank Braynard.

The almost frantic pace of the Hudson waterfront lessened considerably after the sixties. Its piers and slips, however, witnessed what was the most exciting day in recent Port history, Operation Sail, during the Bicentennial celebrations in 1976. Nearly two dozen of the world's largest sailing ships sailed in procession to various berths, escorted by hundreds of pleasure craft, tugs, fireboats, spectator craft, and a sizable fleet of international navy vessels. Several millions watched the festivities from both banks of the river, from skyscraper windows, from apartment tower terraces, and from as far away as the Jersey Palisades. It was unanimously acknowledged as the most spectacular event of the entire national celebration.

The spirit of Operation Sail, though not on quite the same scale, has been kept alive by the Harbor Festival, which is largely underwritten by the Port Authority of New York & New Jersey. Each summer, in the days surrounding the Independence Day holiday, as many as a dozen public events have been staged: a full parade along lower Broadway, lifeboat races, a street fair, dance and music performances, and evening fireworks off Liberty Island. Ten years after the original Operation Sail, a large Harbor Festival is being planned for 1986, honoring the Statue of Liberty's centennial.

Lots of New York harbor's past is alive and well, and much of it easily accessible.

A contrast between the old and new: The USCG barque *Eagle*, sail training vessel for the U.S. Coast Guard, passes the World Trade Center building.

LIST of ILLUSTRATIONS
and CREDITS

(Unless otherwise noted, these photos have been taken by Francis J. Duffy)

198

INDEX